Upper-Interm   ite

New Headway
Pronunciation Course

Bill Bowler
Sarah Cunningham

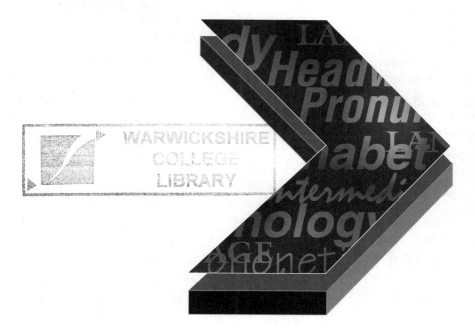

OXFORD
UNIVERSITY PRESS

Contents

Introduction

Welcome to the *New Headway Upper-Intermediate Pronunciation Course*!

The questions and answers on these pages are to help you to understand this book, so that you can get the best out of it when you use it.

Who is this book for?

The New Headway Upper-Intermediate Pronunciation Course is for upper-intermediate level students who wish to improve their English pronunciation.

How does this book work?

You can use this book (and tape) on their own. The exercises in it will help you to organize your study of pronunciation.

It is also part of the *New Headway English Course* and the topics and language of each unit in this book link with those in the *New Headway Upper-Intermediate Student's Book*.

What types of exercise are there?

There are four different types of exercise in this book:

1 **Sounds and spelling** The sounds exercises help you to practise the sounds that we use in English. Some sounds exercises are particularly suitable for speakers of certain languages. (See the table below.) Sounds and spelling exercises deal with the relationship between spelling patterns and sounds. They are suitable for speakers of all languages.

Sounds exercises

Unit		All nationalities	Arabic	Chinese	Czech	French	German	Greek	Hungarian	Italian	Japanese	Polish	Portuguese	Russian	Spanish	Turkish
Unit 1	The sounds /iː/, /ɪ/, or /aɪ/?	✔														
	The silent -e rule	✔														
Unit 2	The sound /h/ and linking /w/ and /j/				✔	✔	✔		✔	✔		✔			✔	✔
	Silent letter *h*	✔														
Unit 3	The sound /r/ in British and American English	✔														
Unit 4	The sounds /əʊ/, /ɔː/ and /ɒ/	✔														
	Pronunciation of the letter *o*	✔														
Unit 5	'Dark' /l/ and 'clear' /l/	✔														
	Silent letter *l*	✔														
Unit 6	The sound /ŋ/ (and /n/, /ŋg/, /ŋk/, and /ndʒ/)					✔				✔	✔		✔			
	Silent letters *g*, *k*, and *n*	✔														
Unit 7	The sounds /θ/, /t/, and /s/	✔														
	Pronunciation of *s* with different spelling patterns	✔														
Unit 8	The sounds /e/, /æ/, and /ʌ/	✔														
	Pronunciation of the letters *e*, *a*, and *u*	✔														
Unit 9	The sounds /ð/, /d/, and /z/	✔														
	The sounds /θ/, /ð/, /t/, /d/, /s/, and /z/	✔														
Unit 10	The sounds /ʃ/, /tʃ/, and /dʒ/		✔	✔		✔	✔	✔		✔		✔		✔		
	Pronunciation of the letters *ch*	✔														
Unit 11	The sounds /v/, and /w/, and silent *w*		✔	✔	✔		✔		✔	✔	✔		✔			✔
	The sounds /b/, and /v/, and silent *b*		✔							✔					✔	
Unit 12	Sound symbol crossword	✔														
	Silent letter round-up	✔														

2 Connected speech These exercises help you to pronounce words in phrases and sentences correctly.

3 Intonation and sentence stress These exercises help you to hear and practise different kinds of intonation and sentence stress patterns.

4 Word focus In these exercises you study groups of words where there are problems with sounds and word stress.

What about the tape?

This book comes with one tape. Some exercises have different sections of tape (a, b, c, etc.). The symbol in the exercise shows exactly which part of the tape you listen to.

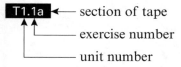

What about the key?

The answers to exercises, and tapescripts which are not in full in the exercises themselves, are in the key at the back of the book.

As in the *New Headway* Student's Book, sometimes we ask you questions to help you work out rules for yourself. The answers to these questions are in the key, too.

The key symbol after an exercise means look at the key. The page number with the key symbol shows you exactly where to look: ⚷ **p. 54**

What about technical words?

Here is a list of technical words we use in this book. Use a bilingual dictionary to translate them. You can look back at this list while you use the book.

consonant _____

contraction _____

flat _____

formal _____

informal _____

intonation _____

linking _____

phonetic _____

polite _____

pronunciation _____

rude _____

sentence _____

sound _____

spelling _____

stress _____

syllable _____

symbol _____

vowel _____

weak _____

The sounds /iː/, /ɪ/, and /aɪ/
The silent -e rule
Pronouns and verbs in fast speech
Hellos and goodbyes
Word families, stress, and the sound /ə/

Sounds and spelling

1 The sounds /iː/, /ɪ/, and /aɪ/

> The pronunciation of many words in English is impossible to work out from the spelling. Listen to these three words to make sure that you can hear the difference between the sounds /iː/, /ɪ/, and /aɪ/ in the <u>underlined</u> syllables.
>
> | | /iː/ | /ɪ/ | /aɪ/ |
> |---|---|---|---|
> | **T1.1a** | <u>pe</u>ople | lan<u>gua</u>ge | <u>i</u>sland |

1 How many of these words can you pronounce correctly?

<u>sce</u>nery   water<u>ski</u>ing   sun<u>shine</u>   <u>busi</u>ness   sup<u>plies</u>
<u>bi</u>lingual   fi<u>nan</u>cial   <u>de</u>cent   en<u>ti</u>rely

T1.1b Listen and check your answers.

2 **T1.1c** How do you pronounce these phrases with nationality adjectives? Listen and write in the symbols /iː/, /ɪ/, or /aɪ/. Practise saying them.

/iː/ /aɪ/
Greek Islands

/ / / // /
Icelandic fishermen

/ / / / / /
Italian ice-cream

/ / / // /
Indian spices

/ // / / // /
Egyptian linen

/ // // /
Chinese silk

/ // / / /
Swedish films

Check your answers. 🔑 **p. 54**

2 The silent -e rule

1 **T1.2a** Listen to these pairs of words. What happens in each case when *e* is added?

A		B	
win		wine	
bit		bite	
mad		made	
Dan		Dane	
hop		hope	
not		note	
pet		Pete	
cut		cute	

Put the correct phonetic symbol next to the words in each column.

/ɪ/ /e/ /ɒ/ /ʌ/ /æ/ /juː/ /aɪ/ /eɪ/ /iː/ /əʊ/

🗝 p. 54

2 Try to guess how these words are pronounced. Use your answers in 1 to help you. Check any new words in your dictionary.

site	rot	pin	mate	mope
fin	slop	cod	cope	pine
dike	rid	kite	spite	whip
spit	shin	spine	obscene	delete

T1.2b Listen and check your answers.

Notice what happens to words with a short vowel sound when a suffix is added:

-ing:	get	→	get**ting**		
	sit	→	sit**ting**		
-ed:	fit	→	fit**ted**		
	hop	→	hop**ped**		
-er / -est:	big	→	big**ger**	→	big**gest**
	hot	→	hot**ter**	→	hot**test**

Notice what happens to words with a long vowel sound when a suffix is added:

-ing:	hate	→	hat**ing**		
	shine	→	shin**ing**		
-ed:	tape	→	tape**d**		
	hope	→	hope**d**		
-er / -est:	late	→	later	→	late**st**
	fine	→	fine**r**	→	fine**st**

---

3 How would you spell these words with the suffixes above them?

-ing	*-ed*	*-er*	*-est*
spit	mope	fit	close
win	whip	cute	thin
cope	note	fat	mad
shop	pop	pale	sad

🗝 p. 54

Connected speech

3 Pronouns and verbs in fast speech

1 Match the dialogues with the pictures.

a '**I'm** sure **we're being** followed, **you** know ... **you** see that black car – **it's been** driving behind us for ages.'
   'Don't **be** ridiculous – why **would** anyone want to follow us? **You're** just **being** paranoid!'
b 'What a mess! What on earth **have you been** doing?'
   '**We were** only trying to make a nice surprise for you ...'
   'Okay, **I'm** sorry ... **we'll** sort it out together, shall we?'
c 'Excuse me, **I was** told **I'd be** seen immediately, and **I've been** waiting for ages now!'
   'The doctors **are** doing their best, but I'm afraid **they're** very busy. **Do you** think **you could** wait over there, please?'

T1.3a Listen and check your answers. Notice the pronunciation of the pronouns and verbs in **bold**. Why are they pronounced like this?

🗝 p. 54

2 Practise the pronunciation. Start with just the pronouns and auxiliaries, then add the rest of the sentence or clause, like this:

/æv bɪn/

I've been → I've been waiting → I've been waiting for ages!

3 **T1.3b** Listen to the dialogue, without reading the text below. Who is it about? What has happened to them? What are they going to do?

4 Read the dialogue. Which pronouns and verbs are missing?

   A Anyway, I suppose _____ heard about Mark and Sonia?

   B No, what?

   A Oh, _____ know? _____ emigrating to New Zealand.

   B Really, how come?

   A I think _____ having a lot of problems lately – you knew their house _____ burgled last year, while _____ asleep in bed?

   B No, _____ actually … how awful!

   A Yeah, and Sonia _____ suffering with her nerves ever since, _____ even off work for a while, I think.

   B Oh no, I had no idea.

   A And now apparently, Mark _____ made redundant from his job!

   B The poor things!

   A I know … so that's why _____ decided to make a fresh start in New Zealand. I think Mark _____ paid quite a lot of redundancy money, so _____ going to start up their own business.

   B Oh … well I hope it works out for them. _____ know when _____ leaving?

   A _____ know but I think _____ going before the end of the month.

   B Oh, right – _____ give them a call to wish them all the best.

   A Yes, _____ sure _____ appreciate that.

Listen again and check your answers.   🔑 **p. 54**

5 Practise the dialogue with a partner. Pay attention to the pronunciation of the pronouns and weak forms.

Intonation

4 Hellos and goodbyes

1 **T1.4a** Listen to these three dialogues. Imagine a situation for each one. How do the people feel towards each other?

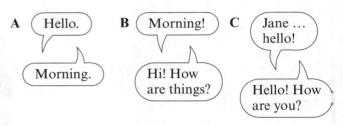

A Hello. / Morning.

B Morning! / Hi! How are things?

C Jane … hello! / Hello! How are you?

What do you notice about the intonation in each case?

2 **T1.4b** Listen to these people greeting each other and mark the dialogues:

   * if they sound neutral or uninterested (like speaker **A** above),

   ** if they sound friendly and interested (like speaker **B** above),

   *** if they sound excited / very pleased to see each other (like speaker **C** above).

1 ☐ 'Hi.'
     'Hi, all right?'

2 ☐ 'Hello. How are you doing?'
     'Fine, thanks … and you?'

3 [ ] 'Morning. What's new?'
'Oh, nothing much. Just the usual.'

4 [ ] 'Hello. Lovely to see you. You look well.'
'You too! How's it going? It's ages since I saw you last!'

5 [ ] 'I'll be off now. See you later.'
'Yeah … see you around.'

6 [ ] 'Bye, I'll be in touch, yeah?'
'Fine, bye.'

 p. 54

Word focus

5 Word families, stress, and the sound /ə/

The strongest syllable in a word is called the stressed syllable. All words have a stressed syllable. In word families this can sometimes change.

● ● ·
a photograph
/ˈfəʊtəgrɑːf/

· ● ● ·
photographic
/ˌfəʊtəˈgræfɪk/

· ● · ·
photographer
/fəˈtɒgrəfə/

· ● ● ·
to photograph
/ˈfəʊtəgrɑːf/

T1.5a Listen to the stress in each word.

1 Look at the phonetic spelling of the words above. Which sound is most common in the **unstressed** syllable? This is the most common vowel sound in English.

2 Listen again and repeat the words, paying attention to the stress and the sound /ə/.

3 Here are some more word families. Mark the main stress and underline the /ə/ sounds.
Which words have no /ə/ sound?

Noun	Adjective	Person	Verb
industry	industrial	industrialist	industrialize
invention	inventive	inventor	invent
competition	competitive	competitor	compete
criticism	critical	critic	criticize
politics	political	politician	politicize
nation	nationalistic	nationalist	nationalize
analysis	analytical	analyst	analyse

T1.5b Listen and check your answers. p. 54

Listen again and practise saying the words that you guessed incorrectly.

2

The sound /h/ and linking /w/ and /j/
Silent letter *h*
Strong and weak forms of prepositions
Exclamations
Stress in phrasal verbs

Sounds and spelling

1 The sound /h/ and linking /w/ and /j/

1 **T2.1a** Listen and tick (✔) the words you hear.

a ☐ hair   ☐ air

b ☐ heat   ☐ eat

c ☐ hearing   ☐ earring

d ☐ heels   ☐ eels

🔑 p. 54

To make the sound /h/, push air out of your mouth without moving your tongue or using your voice.

In English, if we pronounce a word with the sound /h/, we write it with the letter *h*.

T2.1b *hello   holiday   inhabitant*

We do not pronounce the letter *h* when it comes after a vowel at the end of a word.

T2.1c *Ah!   Eh?   Oh!   Deborah*

2 **T2.1d** Listen and repeat these pairs of words, paying attention to the pronunciation of /h/.

hair	air	heart	art
heat	eat	hall	all
hearing	earring	hill	ill
heels	eels		

3 Work in pairs.

Student A Say one of the words in 2.
Student B Point to the word you hear.

Repeat this until Student A has said all the words. Swap over.

In fast speech, when a word begins with a vowel sound, it links with the word before. (Be careful not to add an *h* sound at the start of a word where it isn't needed!)

modern‿art

T2.1e When the word before also ends in a vowel sound, then either a /w/ or a /j/ is added.

/w/
What nice blue‿earrings!

/j/
I love sea‿air.

Circle the correct rules.

> a A *rounded/spread* vowel sound (eg /uː/) at the end of a word is linked to the following word with a /w/ sound.
>
> b A *rounded/spread* vowel sound (eg /iː/) at the end of a word is linked to the following word with a /j/ sound.

4 **T2.1f** Listen to these sentences. <u>Underline</u> the linking /w/ sounds.

a Henry and I agree you are to inherit the antique hatstand.

b Helen was free at seven, and she hurried to meet Joe at the opera house.

c Holly admires my nephew Hugh a lot. He's a handsome boy, and so intelligent too.

Listen again and underline the linking /j/ sounds like this ∿∿. 🔑 p. 54

Practise reading the sentences, paying attention to the pronunciation of *h* and linking /w/ and /j/.

2 Silent letter *h*

1 **T2.2a** Listen to these words. Circle the odd word in each line, and say why it is different.

a heir   honest   hotel   hours
b perhaps   rhyme   rhino   rhythm
c whale   when   whole   white 🔑 p. 54

Listen again and repeat the words.

2 Complete the rules. Use the words in 1 to help you.

> a *h* is usually pronounced at the beginning of words, but it is silent in the words _____, _____, and _____.
>
> b *rh* at the beginning of words is always pronounced _____.
>
> c *wh* at the beginning of words is usually pronounced _____. In words beginning with *who-*, *wh-* is usually pronounced _____. 🔑 p. 55

3 Cross out the silent *h*s in these words.

yoghurt	heritage	exhausted	harmony
exhibition	prehistoric	heirloom	hostel
vehicle	hospital	ghastly	diarrhoea

🔑 p. 55

Connected speech

3 Strong and weak forms of prepositions

1 **T2.3a** Listen and repeat.

a They're from Spain.
b We spoke to Janet.
c It's made of plastic.
d She's waiting for Frank.
e He's looking at Andrea.

2 **T2.3b** Listen and repeat.

a Where are they from?
b Who did we speak to?
c What's it made of?
d Who's she waiting for?
e Who's he looking at?

3 Look at the sentences in 1 and 2. Complete the rules.

> a When a preposition comes at the end of a question, the pronunciation is _____.
>
> b When a preposition comes in the middle of a sentence, the pronunciation is usually _____ in fast speech. 🔑 p. 55

4 **T2.3c** Listen and repeat these questions.

a What's it made of?
b Where's it from?
c What's it for?

5 Listen to the questions again. This time stop the tape after each question and reply, using the words in the boxes. Make sure you pronounce the prepositions weakly.

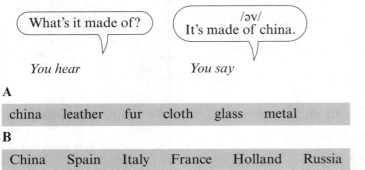

What's it made of?

/əv/
It's made of china.

You hear   *You say*

A

| china | leather | fur | cloth | glass | metal |

B

| China | Spain | Italy | France | Holland | Russia |

C

keeping perfume in	storing food in
putting flowers in	wearing on your head
watering plants	keeping your place in a book

6 Work with a partner. Choose one of the souvenirs from the display cabinet. Your partner must guess which souvenir you are thinking of by asking questions like this:

A What's it made of?
B It's made of metal.
A What's it for?
B It's for watering flowers.

Intonation and sentence stress

4 Exclamations

1 Match each adjective with its opposite in the box.

a some hideous hats
b a disgusting flavour   _____
c a sensible woman   _____
d a stale cake   _____
e a smart jacket   _____
f a gorgeous view   _____
g a cheerful atmosphere   _____
h a varied lifestyle   _____

delicious	ghastly
fresh	foolish
shabby	depressing
monotonous	attractive

T2.4a Listen and check your answers. ☞ p. 55

Listen again and practise saying the pairs of words.

2 Fill in the grid of uncountable and countable nouns. Use the anagrams to help you.

General (uncountable)	**Particular** (countable)	
a advice	_____	nitegusogs
b bread	_____	alfo
c clothes	_____	tifuto
d food	_____	lema
e luggage	_____	cesa
f music	_____	unte
g weather	_____	elitmac
h work	_____	boj

3 Transform these sentences, using a countable noun instead of an uncountable noun.

a What hideous clothes!
What *a hideous outfit*!
b What shabby luggage!
What _____ !
c What gorgeous weather!
What _____ !

Check your answers.  **p. 55**

4 **T2.4b** Listen and repeat these sentences. Make sure your voice rises and falls like this:

What hideous clothes!   What a hideous outfit!

5 **T2.4c** Listen and respond.

delicious meal

What a delicious meal!

What a delicious meal!

You listen   *You speak*   *You listen*

 p. 55

5 Stress in phrasal verbs

> Phrasal verbs, or multi-word verbs, often follow this pattern.
>
> She (put on) **her socks**. (verb + adverb / preposition + *noun object*)
>
> She (put) **her socks** (on). (verb + *noun object* + adverb / preposition)
>
> She (put) **them** (on). (verb + *pronoun object* + adverb / preposition)
>
> She put ~~on them~~. **X**

1 **T2.5a** Listen to these sentences and mark the stress patterns like this ■.

a She put on her shoes.
b She put her shoes on.
c She put them on. **p. 55**

2 Some phrasal verbs have Latin verb synonyms. Match each phrasal verb from the box with an underlined verb in the sentences below. Use a dictionary to help you.

put off	put up	put out	put together
take back	take in		

a Can you <u>return</u> my books to the library? _____
b Let's <u>postpone</u> the party until May. _____
c That DIY desk was hard to <u>assemble</u>. _____
d I can't <u>absorb</u> facts when I'm tired. _____
e They're going to <u>increase</u> income tax. _____
f Please <u>extinguish</u> your cigarettes. _____

3 **T2.5b** Listen and respond, changing the noun object into a pronoun object each time. Pay attention to the stress patterns you marked in 1.

He's put our meeting off.

He's put it off.

He's put it off.

You listen   *You speak*   *You listen*

 **p. 55**

3

The sound /r/ in British and American English
Linking with book and film titles
Rising and falling intonation in questions
Stress in compound adjectives
Opposites with *dis-, il-, im-, in-, ir-,* and *un-*

Sounds

1 The sound /r/ in British and American English

1 Below are ten adjectives that describe personal characteristics. Can you remember what they all mean?

T3.1a Listen to each word in both British and American accents. Mark them with a tick (✔) if *r* is pronounced and a cross (✗) if it is not.

	British	**American**
a	✗ hardwo✗rking	✔ hardwo✔rking
b	reliable	reliable
c	practical	practical
d	sincere	sincere
e	organized	organized
f	proud	proud
g	relaxed	relaxed
h	careless	careless
i	popular	popular

2 Circle the correct rules.

> a When *r* comes before a vowel sound, it:
>   *is / is not* pronounced in British English.
>   *is / is not* pronounced in American English.
> b When *r* comes after a vowel sound, it:
>   *is / is not* pronounced in British English.
>   *is / is not* pronounced in American English.
>
> p. 55

Practise saying the adjectives in 1. You can say them in either the British or American way, but make sure that you pronounce /r/ correctly.

3 How do you think these adjectives are pronounced in British English?

extrovert	warm-hearted	superior
self-centred	cheerful	good-natured
particular	short-tempered	

T3.1b Listen to see if you guessed correctly.

4 The *r* at the end of a word or syllable is also sometimes pronounced in British English.

T3.1c Listen to these adjectives and say when the *r* in *over-* is pronounced and when it is not.

over-modest	over-careful	over-excited
over-qualified	overpaid	over-ambitious
over-confident	over-educated	

 p. 55

Listen again and practise saying the adjectives.

 p. 55

5 What is the special meaning of *over-* in these words? With a partner, invent a sentence for each word.

6 **T3.1d** Listen to the dialogue between Matthew and Laura. Mark the linking *r* sounds.

Laura Matthew! Are you going anywhere over Easter this year?

Matthew Well, yes, as a matter of fact, we are. We're off on a tour of Italy for a week or two.

Laura Mmm. That sounds great! Where exactly will you be going?

Matthew Oh, here and there. Rome's more or less definite, but we're open to suggestions.

Laura Are you travelling by coach?

Matthew No, by car actually.

Laura When you're in Rome, you must throw a coin over your shoulder into the Trevi fountain.

Matthew Really? What for?

Laura It means, sooner or later, you're sure to return.

 p. 55

Practise the dialogue with a partner, paying attention to the *r* sounds.

Connected speech

2 Linking with book and film titles

1 Look at the film titles. Have you seen any of them? What did you think of them? Who starred in them?

> When a word begins with a vowel sound, and the previous word ends in a consonant, the two words link:
>
> Four Weddings and a Funeral
>
> Silence of the Lambs
>
> Three Men and a Baby
>
> Home Alone
>
> Raiders of the Lost Ark
>
> Sister Act
>
> Shakespeare in Love
>
> As Good as it Gets
>
> **T3.2a** Listen and repeat. Practise the linking.

2 Below are the titles of some famous English novels. Mark the words that link together.

> **The Mayor of Casterbridge**
>
> **Pride and Prejudice**
>
> *Alice in Wonderland*
>
> Jane Eyre
>
> *Great Expectations*
>
> **The Hound of the Baskervilles**

T3.2b Listen and check your answers. **p. 56**

Practise saying the titles with the word linking.

Intonation

3 Rising and falling intonation in questions

1 **T3.3a** Ellen is being interviewed for a job as a holiday representative. Listen to part of the interview and number the questions in the order you hear them.

a ☐ So how did you learn French?
b ☐ You spent two summers working on a farm?
c ☐ What about previous work experience?
d ☐ And you'd like to work in Greece? ↗
e ☐ Are you old enough to work in a casino?
f ☐ Do you speak any other languages at all?
g ☐ In a casino?
h ☐ Which other languages did you say you speak?
i ☐ Why Greece?
j ☐ Do you speak Spanish well?
k ☐ What other jobs have you done?
l ☐ Do you speak Greek?

Check your answers. **p. 56**

What did you find out about Ellen from her answers? Do you think she got the job?

2 **T3.3b** Listen to the interview questions on their own. Mark them like this ➚ if the intonation goes up at the end and like this ➘ if it goes down.

In Yes / No questions, or in statements that are made into questions, the intonation normally goes **up** at the end:

Do you speak Greek? ➚

You spent two summers working on a farm? ➚

In *Wh-* questions, the intonation normally goes **down** at the end:

So how did you learn French? ➘   *Why Greece?* ➘

Sometimes we repeat a question because we have forgotten the answer, or were surprised by the answer. In these cases, the intonation goes up at the end:

And which other languages did you say you speak? ➚

In a casino? ➚

T3.3c To practise the intonation, try humming the questions first like this:

☐   ☐ ■➘

mm MM mm mm MM MM?

☐   ☐ ■➘

So how did you learn French?

☐   ☐ ■➚

mm mm MM mm MM mm MM?

☐   ☐ ■➚

And you'd like to work in Greece?

Practise saying all the questions in 1.

3 Look at the tapescript on page 56. Read it aloud with a partner, paying attention to the intonation.

Word focus

4 Stress in compound adjectives

1 Put the words from boxes **A** and **B** together to make compound adjectives to fit the definitions below.

A

well-	badly-	self-	left-
over	broad-	quick-	good-

B

minded	centred	handed	looking
weight	tempered	behaved	dressed

a A person who writes with their left hand is ***left-handed***.
b A person who only thinks about what they want rather than what other people want is _____ .
c A person who doesn't wear neat or clean clothes is _____ .
d Children who do what adults think they should do are _____ .
e Someone who often gets angry without having a good reason is _____ .
f A person who is fatter than they should be is _____ .
g A person who accepts behaviour that some people might disapprove of is _____ .
h If someone is attractive physically, you can say he or she is _____ .

2 **T3.4a** Listen and check your answers. As you listen, mark the **main** stress on the compound adjectives. 🔑 p. 56

3 Match the pictures with the adjectives in 1.

Notice the stress pattern. When the adjectives are not followed by a noun, the main stress is on the second word:

●   ●
self-centred   broad-minded

However, there is also secondary stress on the first word:

● ●   ● ●
self-centred   broad-minded

In a dictionary, main stress is marked like this ' and secondary stress is marked like this ,.

,self-'centred   ,broad-'minded

Listen again and repeat the adjectives from 1, paying attention to stress.

4   **T3.4b** Here are some more compound adjectives. Can you work out what they mean? Practise saying them, paying attention to the stress.

long-suffering	self-pitying
kind-hearted	broad-shouldered
narrow-minded	self-confident
badly-behaved	self-conscious
well-dressed	right-handed

5   Work in pairs. Discuss the adjectives above and those in 1 like this:

> Being broad-minded is a good thing to be.

> Being quick-tempered is a bad thing to be.

> Being left-handed is neither good nor bad.

> Being self-centred might be positive if you are an ambitious politician or a talented artist, for example.

5 Opposites with *dis-, il-, im-, in-, ir-,* and *un-*

1   To make opposites, we often use the prefixes *dis-, il-, im-, in-, ir-,* and *un-*. Write in the opposites of these adjectives. Use a dictionary to help you.

a	____honest	f	____formal	k	____correct
b	____reliable	g	____legal	l	____reasonable
c	____polite	h	____satisfied	m	____responsible
d	____rational	i	____logical	n	____acceptable
e	____mature	j	____moral	o	____possible

 p. 56

2   Complete the rules.

> a   We often use *im-* with words beginning with the letters ____ or ____ .
> b   We often use *il-* with words beginning with the letter ____ .
> c   We often use *ir-* with words beginning with the letter ____ .
>
> Notice that there are many adjectives which do not follow these rules, e.g. *unpleasant, disloyal, unrealistic*.

 p. 56

3   Put the opposites from 1 into the correct column in the table.

● ● ●	● ● ●	● ● ● ● ●	● ● ● ●
dishonest	impolite	unreliable	irrational

T3.5a Listen and check your answers.   p. 56

Listen again and practise saying the words with the correct stress.

4   Write sentences to show the meaning of five opposites from 1.

Example
It's going to be quite an informal party, so there's no need to dress up.

5   Work with a partner.
Student A Read out your example sentences, but say *fizzbuzz* each time instead of the adjective.

Example

> It's going to be quite a fizzbuzz party, so there's no need to dress up.

Student B Listen and guess the adjective. Swap over.

The sounds /əʊ/, /ɔ:/, and /ɒ/
Pronunciation of the letter *o*
Sentences with and without the indefinite article
Wh- questions with up intonation
Homographs

Sounds and spelling

1 The sounds /əʊ/, /ɔ:/, and /ɒ/

1 **T4.1a** Listen to these words. Make sure that you can hear the difference between the <u>underlined</u> vowel sounds.

a b<u>oa</u>t   b airp<u>or</u>t   c l<u>o</u>rry

2 **T4.1b** Listen to these words. Sort them according to the <u>underlined</u> sounds.

b<u>ow</u>ls   c<u>o</u>ffee   cl<u>o</u>thes   str<u>aw</u>berries
tomat<u>oe</u>s   c<u>or</u>n   <u>o</u>live oil   precious st<u>o</u>nes
cl<u>o</u>th   tobacc<u>o</u>   p<u>o</u>ttery   footb<u>a</u>lls
c<u>o</u>c<u>oa</u>   g<u>o</u>ld   s<u>au</u>sages   s<u>o</u>ft drinks

on the boat /əʊ/	at the airport /ɔ:/	on the lorry /ɒ/

Which method of transport has the longest list? Which has the shortest?

🔑 p. 56

2 Pronunciation of the letter *o*

1 **T4.2a** Listen to these sounds and words. Circle the word in each group where the pronunciation of the letter *o* does not match the sound on the left.

a /ʌ/   money   love   others   both
b /əʊ/   women   woken   woven   ago
c /ə/   police   polish   complain   pollute
d /ɒ/   gone   on   done   soft
e /u:/   who   lose   do   whole

🔑 p. 57

Listen again and repeat the sounds and words. Pay attention to the pronunciation of the letter *o*.

2 Look at these sentences. Tick (✔) the box if the <u>underlined</u> words rhyme. Cross (✘) the box if the <u>underlined</u> words do not rhyme.

a ☐ It got <u>lost</u> in the <u>post</u>.
b ☐ Have you got any <u>money</u>, <u>honey</u>?
c ☐ This <u>shoe</u> hurts my <u>toe</u>.
d ☐ Don't <u>bother</u> about my <u>brother</u>.
e ☐ He put the <u>rose</u> to his <u>nose</u>.
f ☐ She was a famous <u>Roman</u> <u>woman</u>.

🔑 p. 57

3 **T4.2b** Listen and repeat the sentences. Pay attention to the pronunciation of the <u>underlined</u> words.

3 Sentences with and without the indefinite article

1 **T4.3a** Look at these pairs of sentences. Listen and tick (✔) the sentences you hear.

a ☐ That's very beautiful glass.
b ☐ That's a very beautiful glass.

c ☐ How much is coffee in New York?
d ☐ How much is a coffee in New York?

e ☐ Do you want gold?
f ☐ Do you want a gold?

g ☐ I've got few friends in my new class.
h ☐ I've got a few friends in my new class.

i ☐ What lovely lamb!
j ☐ What a lovely lamb!

k ☐ This is fascinating work.
l ☐ This is a fascinating work.

🔑 p. 57

2 Read all the sentences aloud.

3 Match each sentence above with one of these responses.

1 ☐ *b* Yes, it's for champagne, I think.
2 ☐ Well, you certainly seem pleased with your job.
3 ☐ Oh, dear. You poor thing. You must be very lonely.
4 ☐ Yes. He was born only a few hours ago.
5 ☐ It's fallen – like most things on the New York commodities index.
6 ☐ Well, I got a silver medal at the last Olympics, so yes.
7 ☐ Yes. I think that would look nice in the bathroom window.
8 ☐ Well, you make friends wherever you go, don't you?
9 ☐ Mmm. Isn't it delicious?
10 ☐ Yes. It's one of Shakespeare's early plays, isn't it?
11 ☐ A couple of dollars maybe.
12 ☐ Oh yes, I'm allergic to silver.

🔑 p. 57

4 Work in pairs.
Student A Read a sentence from 1 aloud.
Student B Reply with the appropriate response from 3.
Swap over.

Intonation and sentence stress

4 *Wh-* questions with up intonation

As you saw in Unit 3, the intonation usually goes down at the end of *Wh-* questions.

Adele What's your name?
Eric Eric Gruber.

T4.4a However, when we ask someone to repeat information that was unclear at first hearing, the intonation goes up. Listen.

Adele I'm Adele Felaanava.

Eric What's your name?
Adele Adele Felaanava.

---

1 **T4.4b** Listen to these phone dialogues between Adele, a visitor from England, and Eric, an Australian businessman. Pay attention to the question words. Stop the tape at each tone. Decide if Adele is going to repeat something or add new information.

Eric Why are you phoning?
Adele To speak to you.
Eric Why?
TONE
Adele To speak to you. / To get a job.

Eric Where are you from?
Adele England.
Eric Where?
TONE
Adele England. / Manchester.

🔑 p. 57

2 **T4.4c** Take Adele's part in the conversation.

When Eric first asks a question, give response 1.

Listen carefully as Eric repeats the question word:
If the intonation goes up, repeat response 1.
If the intonation goes down, give response 2 (the new information).

Listen to the correct response.

a When did you arrive?
  1 Last week.
  2 Last Monday.
b Why did you leave England?
  1 I was unemployed.
  2 I'd been made redundant.
c How many contacts have you got here?
  1 Quite a few.
  2 One or two.
d How long are you staying?
  1 Just a short time.
  2 A couple of months.
e How did you get my phone number?
  1 Just by chance.
  2 From a friend.
f What are you interested in?
  1 A job in sales.
  2 Selling make-up.

🔑 p. 57

3 Work in pairs. Use the prompts in 2 to perform a new dialogue between Adele and Eric in the same way, using repeated question words and varying your intonation.

Word focus

5 Homographs

T4.5a Homographs are words that are spelt the same, but which have different pronunciation and a different use or meaning. Listen.

When you want to record something, press this button. (record = verb)

And this amazing athlete has just broken another world record! (record = noun)

The stress pattern is the same if a noun is used as an adjective:

I work for a record company. (record = noun used as an adjective)

1 **T4.5b** Listen to each sentence and circle the word you hear.

a 1 rebel   2 rebel

b 1 contract   2 contract

c 1 rebel   2 rebel

d 1 contract   2 contract

e 1 rebel   2 rebel

f 1 contract   2 contract

🔑 p. 57

2 Circle the correct rules about two-syllable homographs.

In two-syllable homographs:

a *nouns / verbs* are usually stressed ● •.

b *nouns / verbs* are usually stressed • ●.

3 Match the phonetic transcriptions from the box below with the underlined words in these sentences.

a ☐ The present had a big pink bow on the top.

b ☐ He gave a low bow to the audience.

c ☐ Close the door, please.

d ☐ You're too close to the microphone.

e ☐ The road wound up the hill.

f ☐ He had a nasty wound on his leg.

g ☐ She bathed the baby and put him to bed.

h ☐ I bathed my cut finger in antiseptic solution.

1 /baʊ/	5 /waʊnd/
2 /bəʊ/	6 /wuːnd/
3 /kləʊs/	7 /beɪðd/
4 /kləʊz/	8 /bɑːθt/

🔑 p. 57

4 **T4.5c** Listen and repeat the sentences. Make sure you pronounce the homographs correctly.

5 Write some crazy sentences with other pairs of homographs that you know. Practise reading them aloud.

'Dark' /l/ and 'clear' /l/
Silent letter *l*
Linking with *and* in common phrases
Special stress
Words ending in *-ion*

Sounds and spelling

1 'Dark' /l/ and 'clear' /l/

1 **T5.1a** Listen to these phrases. Write **1** next to the first phrase you hear and **2** next to the second phrase.

a ☐ a man who's bored ☐ a man who's bald

b ☐ some children rowing ☐ some children rolling

c ☐ an impossible code ☐ an impossible cold

d ☐ a strange word ☐ a strange world

e ☐ someone being ☐ someone being
   towed off   told off

🔑 p. 57

2 Listen again, paying attention to the /l/ sound. Does it sound the same as in your language?

> The letter *l* has two pronunciations in English. When there is a **vowel sound** after it, it is a 'clear' /l/:
>
> ***lea*p** /liːp/
>
> When it is at the end of the word, or there is a **consonant sound** after it, it is a 'dark' /l/:
>
> *pee**l*** /piːl/   *pee**led*** /piːld/
>
> **T5.1b** Listen to the three words above. Can you hear the difference between 'clear' /l/ and 'dark' /l/? Practise saying the words.

3 The sounds in the pair of words below are 'back to front'. Look:

/liːp/   /piːl/
leap   peel

Write a word from the box next to each word below to make similar pairs.

| pill | tile | kill | tell |
| feel | kneel | sell | till |

a leaf   *feel*   e lick   _____
b less   _____   f lip   _____
c lit   _____   g light _____
d lean   _____   h let   _____

T5.1c Listen and check your answers. Practise saying the pairs of words making a difference between 'clear' /l/ and 'dark' /l/.

🔑 p. 57

2 Silent letter *l*

1 The letter *l* before a consonant is sometimes silent. Cross out the silent *l*s in these words.

a (half
_____
_____)

b (walk
_____
_____)

c (calm
_____
_____)

d (folk
_____
_____)

e (cold
_____
_____)

f (would
_____
_____)

g (shoulder
_____
_____)

🔑 **p. 57**

2 Below are some more words. Try to guess how they are pronounced. Use the words in 1 to help you. Check any new words in your dictionary.

bold	boulder	calf	chalk	could
fold	mould	palm	psalm	should
stalk	yolk	on behalf of …		

T5.2 Listen and check your answers. How many did you guess correctly?

3 Write the words from 2 in the correct circle in 1 above, according to the sound and spelling. Practise saying the groups of words, paying attention to the silent *l*s and the vowel sounds.

🔑 **p. 57**

Connected speech

3 Linking with *and* in common phrases

1 Put the jumbled words below in the correct order.

a look / found / and / I've / come / what

b decided / see / I've / happens / to / and / wait / what

c go / manager / I'll / ask / the / and / OK / just / that's / if

d I've / I'll / help / when / you / and / this / try / finished

e soon / come / must / and / again / us / you / see

f letter / I'll / post / just / and / go / this

g taxi / phone / try / think / and / I / I'll / a

T5.3a Listen and check your answers. **p. 57**

In informal speech, *and* is often used between two verbs like this:

come and look   wait and see   go and ask   try and help

come and see   go and post   try and phone

Because these verbs are usually said together very quickly, the words link, and some sounds are not pronounced:

come and look   wait and see   go and ask   try and help

T5.3b Listen to the phrases on their own, and practise saying them quickly, as on the tape.

2 ◀ **T5.3a** Listen to the full sentences again. Can you say them as fast as the people on the tape?

3 **T5.3c** Here are some more common phrases with *and*. Listen and practise saying them quickly.

more and more   better and better

worse and worse   **up and down**

in and out   backwards and forwards

on and on   odds and ends

pros and cons   *now and again*

4 Complete the sentences below with the phrases in 3.
a We need to think carefully about the _____ of each possibility.
b Don has to visit a lot of clients, so he's _____ of the office all day long.
c _____ people need to learn English for their jobs.
d I'm fed up of running _____ these stairs!
e We haven't got much food in the house – just a few _____.
f Communication technology is getting _____ all the time.
g The professor's speech went _____ – everyone was bored to death!
h The traffic in town is getting _____ – they'll have to do something about it soon.
i I'll be very pleased when we move nearer to where I work – I'm sick of travelling _____ on the train everyday.
j We don't really go out much these days, but we go to the theatre _____.

🔑— p. 57

Practise reading the sentences aloud, linking the words together.

Stress and intonation

4 Special stress

1 **T5.4a** Listen and <u>underline</u> the word or words with special stress in the second line of each short dialogue below.

a 'Have Ben and Ellen gone home?'
   'Ben has, but I think Ellen's still here.'

b 'I'm sorry I can't go shopping with you this afternoon – I've still got a lot of work to do.'
   'You could go if you wanted to!'

c 'What's the matter? You look really fed up.'
   'I'm just so annoyed with Philip, you'll never guess what he's done now …'

d 'Is this your coat?'
   'No, that one's mine.'

🔑— p. 57

2 In which dialogue is the special stress used to:
   ☐ disagree strongly with someone?
   ☐ contrast two different situations?
   ☐ contradict someone?
   ☐ emphasize something?   🔑— p. 57

Practise the dialogues, paying attention to the special stress.

3 Work with a partner. Read aloud the dialogues below, and decide which of **B**'s words is specially stressed (there may be more than one).

a **A** That's $5, please.
  B It said $4 on the sign over there!

b **A** Do you enjoy beach holidays?
  B I do, and the children do – but my husband doesn't very much, he gets bored.

c **A** Wasn't that new comedy show on Channel 4 last night good?
  B It was hilarious, wasn't it? We were killing ourselves with laughing!

d **A** It's no good, I'll never pass this exam!
  B You might, if you did a bit of studying.

e **A** Oh no, the light bulb's gone!
  B Not again! I only changed it last week!

f **A** You're thirty-four this birthday, aren't you?
  B Thirty-five, unfortunately!

g **A** Laura, you're not watching television, you haven't finished your homework yet.
  B I will finish it, honestly, Mum … later …

h **A** Thank you for having us.
  B Thank you for coming!

4 **T5.4b** Listen and compare your answers with those on the tape. Practise the dialogues, copying the stress and intonation.
🔑 p. 57

Word focus

5 Words ending in *-ion*

1 Check the meaning of any new words below in a dictionary. Where is the stress in each word?

profession	promotion	instruction
fashion	conclusion	occupation
question	completion	emotion
solution	option	communication

T5.5a Listen and check your answers.

2 What do you notice about the position of the stress? How is *-ion* pronounced in English?
🔑 p. 57

Listen again and practise saying the words correctly. Try starting with the stressed syllable like this:

●   ●   ●
pation   cupation   occupation

3 Sometimes the vowel sound in the stressed syllable of *-ion* words is short: /æ/, /e/, /ɒ/, or /ʌ/. Sometimes it is long: /eɪ/, /iː/, /əʊ/, or /uː/.
Complete the table with the words in 1.

	short	long	
a	/æ/		/eɪ/

	short	long	
e	/e/		/iː/

	short	long	
o	/ɒ/		/əʊ/

	short	long	
u	/ʌ/		/uː/

🔑 p. 57

4 Can you see a pattern? Look at the number of consonants between the stressed vowel and *-ion*.
🔑 p. 58

5 Work out the pronunciation of the following words.

consumption	deduction	fraction
passion	explosion	inspection
devotion	adoption	lotion
reception	confusion	inflation
persuasion	completion	contribution

T5.5b Listen and check your answers.

Listen again and practise saying the words.

6

The sound /ŋ/
Silent letters *g*, *k*, and *n*
Unpronounced plosives
Sentence phrasing
-ed adjectives

Sounds and spelling

1 The sound /ŋ/ (and /n/, /ŋg/, /ŋk/, and /ndʒ/)

T6.1a Listen and make sure that you can hear the difference between these three words.

ran   rang   rank

1   **T6.1b** Listen and circle the word you hear.

a	thin	thing	think
b	win	wing	wink
c	pin	ping	pink
d	sin	sing	sink
e	ban	bang	bank
f	banner	banger	banker

 p. 58

> To make the sound /n/, touch the roof of your mouth with your tongue. The air comes out of your nose.
>
> To make the sound /ŋ/, Move your tongue far back in your mouth and then try to say /n/.
>
> In English, if we pronounce a word with the sound /ŋ/, we write it with the letters *ng* or the letter *n* followed by *k* or hard *c*.
>
> **T6.1c** string   skating-rink   incredible

2   ◀ **T6.1b** Listen again and repeat the words in 1. Make sure the difference between the sounds /n/ and /ŋ/ is clear. Don't add a /g/ or a /k/ sound to the end of the words ending in /ŋ/.

3   Work in pairs.

Student A Say one of the words in 1.
Student B Point to the word you hear.

Repeat this until Student A has said all the words. Swap over.

4   Work in pairs. Put the sentences below into the correct order. There may be more than one possibility.

a   skating-rink / Birmingham / at a / while dancing / Aunt Angela / a tango / her ankle / banged / with Uncle Frank / .

_____

b   at the pretty young woman / in a singles' bar / winked / drinking gin / the Hong Kong banker / romantic songs / who was singing / .

_____

c   tongue / pink stringy thing / Angus King's / incredibly long / what's that / on / ?

_____

T6.1d Listen and compare your answers to the tape.

5   Listen again and <u>underline</u> any words or names spelt with *ng* where the *g* is pronounced /g/.   p. 58

Practise saying the sentences correctly.

6   **T6.1e** Listen and put the words into the correct column below according to the pronunciation of *-nger*.

singer	finger	challenger	banger
anger	danger	stronger	ginger
stranger	hanger	plunger	longer

/ŋə/	/ŋgə/	/ndʒə/
singer	*anger*	*stranger*

 p. 58

Practise saying the words correctly.

2 Silent letters *g*, *k*, and *n*

1 Circle the word in each line which does not have a silent letter like the others.

a silent *g*: foreign   signature   gnome   sign
b silent *k*: knot   knight   banknote   know
c silent *n*: hymn   solemn   condemn   autumnal

T6.2a Listen and check your answers.   p. 58

Practise saying the words with silent *g*, *k*, and *n*. Take care not to sound the silent letters.

2 Complete the rules.

> a When the letters *gn* come at the _____ or the _____ of a word – but not the middle – *g* is silent. (Some words with suffixes – like *foreigner*, *signing*, *resigned* – also contain silent 'g' in the middle of the word.)
>
> b When the letter *k* comes before the letter _____ at the beginning of a word, *k* is silent.
>
> c When the letter *n* comes after the letter _____ at the end of a word, *n* is silent.

p. 58

3 Look at the phonetic transcriptions and write the words. They all contain silent *g*, *k*, or *n*.

a /niːl/   _____
b /ˈɔːtəm/   _____
c /ˈfɒrənə/   _____
d /ˈkɒləm/   _____
e /ˈnɒlɪdʒ/   _____
f /ˈsaɪnɪŋ/   _____

T6.2b Listen and check your answers.   p. 58

Listen again and practise saying the words.

Connected speech

3 Unpronounced plosives /d/, /b/, /g/, /t/, /p/, and /k/

> Often, when a plosive sound – /d/, /b/, /g/, /t/, /p/, and /k/ – follows another made with the same mouth position in fast speech, we don't pronounce the first sound.

1 **T6.3a** Listen. Can you hear a difference between the two phrases in each pair?

old oar   old door

her bread   herb bread

big lobe   big globe

right eye   right tie

top layer   top player

black ape   black cape

2 Listen again and practise saying the phrases correctly.

3 **T6.3b** Listen and cross out the examples of silent /d/, /b/, /g/, /t/, /p/, and /k/ in these sentences.

a Rose is our youngest daughter.

b She's wearing a red T-shirt.

c It's a big computer company.

d His alarm clock goes off at eight.

e I love ripe bananas!

f What are my job prospects?

 p. 58

Listen again and practise saying the sentences correctly.

Intonation and sentence stress

4 Sentence phrasing

Look at these sentences.

a Our son, who's studying at Cambridge, wants to be a writer.
(= non-defining relative clause)

This means we have one son. The relative clause gives extra information about him.

b Our son who's studying at Cambridge wants to be a writer.
(= defining relative clause)

This means we have more than one son. The relative clause defines which son we are talking about.

When we write, we use commas to show a non-defining relative clause. When we speak, we use pauses and a different pitch to show a non-defining relative clause. Listen and compare the phrasing in these sentences.

T6.4a

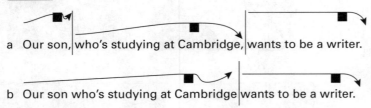

a Our son, who's studying at Cambridge, wants to be a writer.

b Our son who's studying at Cambridge wants to be a writer.

1 **T6.4b** You will hear these sentences said in two different ways, as in the box above. Stop the tape after the tone, and write each sentence with the correct punctuation.

1 I got a card from my aunt who lives in paris

a _____

b _____

2 the computer which we bought in july was stolen

a _____

b _____

3 the uk car plant employees who protested lost their jobs

a _____

b _____

4 jason wanted to prepare a meal which was unusual

a _____

b _____

 p. 58

2 Work in pairs. Discuss the difference in meaning between the a and b sentences.

 p. 58

3 Listen again and practise saying the sentences with the correct intonation and phrasing.

Word focus

5 -ed adjectives + /d/, /t/, and /ɪd/ (and exceptions)

1 Complete the cartoons with the phrases from the box.

I'm bored.	I'm embarrassed.
She's disgusted.	I'm disappointed.
I'm worried.	We're shocked.

a

b

c

T6.5a Listen and check your answers. Listen again and repeat the sentences with feeling. p. 58

2 Put the adjectives from 1 into the correct column according to the pronunciation of -ed.

/d/	/t/	/ɪd/

p. 58

3 Look at the table in 2 and complete the rules.

> a When -ed follows the sound /d/ or /t/, it is pronounced _____.
>
> b When -ed follows a voiceless consonant sound apart from /t/ (= /p/, /k/, /f/, /s/, /θ/, /ʃ/, /tʃ/), it is pronounced _____.
>
> c When -ed follows a vowel sound, or a voiced consonant sound apart from /d/ (= /b/, /g/, /v/, /z/, /ð/, /ʒ/, /dʒ/, /m/, /n/, /ŋ/, /l/, /r/), it is pronounced _____.
>
> p. 58
>
> There are some adjectives which do not follow these rules. They have -ed endings which are pronounced /ɪd/.

4 Complete the sentences with the adjectives from the box.

naked	ragged	wicked
rugged	beloved	jagged

a In the middle of the forest was a house made of chocolate. It belonged to a _____ witch who ate children.

b A poor, hungry-looking girl in a _____ dress was standing on the corner, begging.

c He threw off all his clothes and jumped _____ into the lake.

d The coastline was very _____ at that point – stones and rocks everywhere and the only road was a donkey path.

e Queen Victoria went into mourning and wore only black after the death of her _____ husband Albert in 1867.

f There were a few bits of _____ glass left in the window frame. Clearly the burglar had broken the kitchen window in order to get into the house.

T6.5b Listen and check your answers. p. 58

Listen again and repeat the words.

The sounds /θ/, /t/, and /s/
Pronunciation of *s* with different spelling patterns
Linking in phrases with *get*
Stress in compounds with nouns and adjectives
Stress in multi-word verbs and nouns

Sounds

1 The sounds /θ/, /t/, and /s/

1 **T7.1a** The sound /θ/ is often pronounced wrongly, as /t/ or /s/. Do you have this sound in your language? Listen and make sure you can hear the difference between these three words.

/θ/	/t/	/s/
thank	tank	sank

2 **T7.1b** Listen and circle the word you hear twice.

a	thigh	tie	sigh
b	thick	tick	sick
c	theme	team	seem
d	path	part	pass
e	tenth	tent	tense
f	fourth	fought	force

⚷ p. 58

Practise saying the words, making sure that the difference between them is clear.

If you have problems with the sound /θ/ put your finger in front of your mouth and touch it with your tongue, like this:

3 Write ten words from 2 above. (You can use the same word more than once). Dictate them to your partner, then compare lists. If they are different, what was the problem?

4 **T7.1c** Listen and read the dialogue below. Concentrate on the pronunciation of /θ/, /s/, and /t/.

Simon Kathy! Have you got anything planned for Thursday?

Kathy This Thursday?

Simon Yes, Thursday the thirteenth, it's my birthday.

Kathy Your birthday! I thought it was the thirteenth of *next* month!

Simon No, it's this Thursday. I'm thirty this year, so …

Kathy Thirty … never! I thought you were only about twenty-five!

Simon Thanks! Anyway, I thought we could go out for a meal, or do something to celebrate! Do you think you'll be able to?

Kathy Thursday the thirteenth … let me think … no, that should be fine, I can't think of anything else that's happening.

Simon Well, let's say about six then. I'll tell the others … and have a think about where to go.

Kathy Great. Thanks for inviting me – I'll see you then, then.

Practise the dialogue with a partner.

2 Pronunciation of *s* with different spelling patterns

The letter *s* can be pronounced in four different ways.

	/s/	/z/	/ʃ/	/ʒ/
T7.2a	chase	result	sure	usually

1 **T7.2b** Listen to these common letter combinations with *s*. How is *s* pronounced in each group?

a ☐ *-sion* conclusion decision television

b ☐ *-ose* expose rose chose

c ☐ *-ease* grease cease increase

d ☐ *-sure* measure leisure exposure

e ☐ *dis-* dishonest disappointed disagreement

🔑 p. 58

Practise saying the words.

2 Look at these groups of words. Look at exercise 1. How do you expect *s* to be pronounced? Copy the symbol.

a ☐ confusion revision expansion extension

b ☐ enclose hose pose dose

c ☐ release disease tease decrease

d ☐ insure treasure enclosure pleasure

e ☐ disturb dislike disaster display

T7.2c Listen and cross out the word(s) in each group which do not follow the pattern.

3 How is *s* pronounced in the words you crossed out? Listen again and write the correct symbol above the word.

In which letter combinations is the pronunciation of *s* always, or nearly always, the same?

🔑 p. 59

4 Work with a partner. Use your imagination to make sentences which use at least two of the words above.

I need to measure the television.

I was disappointed by the decision.

Please release the treasure.

Connected speech

3 Linking in phrases with *get*

1 **T7.3a** Listen to the dialogues. Stop the tape at each tone and write in the missing words. Play the tape again if necessary.

a _____ !
Good, I hate school.

b _____ ?
Because you can't read the map.

c Do you like your new job then?
_____ .

d You're late!
_____ .

e _____?
    Yeah, sure.

f _____?
    I think I'll have a beer, please.

 p. 59

The different expressions with *get* show the forms of
linking you have already practised. In Unit 3 you
studied consonant to vowel linking:

T7.3b get‿in   get‿away

In Unit 6 you looked at unpronounced sounds:

T7.3c get̸ready   get̸lost

---

2 **T7.3d** Listen and repeat these phrases, paying
attention to the pronunciation of *get*.

a **get out**   f **get lost**

b *get away*   g **get inside**

c get back   h get down

d **get off**   i *get up*

e get dressed   j *get ready*

3 Look back at the dialogues in 1. Write new ones and
read them aloud, with a partner if possible, paying
attention to the pronunciation of *get*.

Word focus

4 Stress in compounds with nouns and adjectives

1 Match words in boxes **A** and **B** below to make the
objects shown in the pictures. Write the words under
the pictures.

a *mobile phone* _____   e _____

b _____   f _____

c _____   g _____

d _____   h _____

A

portable	personal	electric	mobile
answering	tin	vacuum	cork

B

screw	phone	machine	TV
cleaner	opener	kettle	stereo

2 **T7.4a** Listen and check your answers. As you listen,
mark the stressed syllables, as in the example.

 p. 59

Listen again and practise saying the compound nouns.

There are two types of compound noun. Notice the
different stress patterns:

a noun/gerund + noun   b adjective + noun

  ●   ●   ●
  corkscrew   mobile phone

  ●
  answering machine

---

3 Mark the stress in these compound nouns.

a headphones   g digital television

b computer game   h central heating

c coffee maker   i CD player

d electric razor   j video recorder

e dishwasher   k fan heater

f washing machine

T7.4b Listen and check your answers. ☞ **p. 59**

Practise saying the compound nouns with the correct stress.

4 Discuss these questions with a partner. Which of the things above:
- do you already own?
- would you like to own?
- do you often have problems with? Why?

5 Stress in multi-word verbs and nouns

Sometimes multi-word verbs have an equivalent noun form:

1 to break in   2 a break-in

1 Write in the noun equivalents of the following.

a to get together   _____
b to look out   _____
c to break down   _____
d to get away   _____
e to take off   _____
f to sell out   _____
g to round up   _____

2 Complete the pairs of sentences with a verb or noun form of the multi-word verbs in 1. Use a dictionary to help you if necessary. Put the verbs into the correct form.

a They've had another _**break-in**_ next door.
Did they _**break in**_ through the back window?

b _____ for pickpockets in the city centre, won't you?
Keep a _____ for a parking space!

c The concert was a complete _____, there wasn't a single ticket left.
I wanted to buy a camera like yours, but unfortunately they've _____.

d We must _____ and go out for a drink – I haven't seen you for ages.
At Christmas time, we always have a big family _____.

e As everyone knows, _____ and landing are the most dangerous parts of a flight.
I must admit, I always feel a bit nervous when we're _____ and landing.

f He normally _____ his lectures by asking if we've got any questions.
At four-thirty there will be a brief _____ of the news.

g It's believed that the thieves _____ with several million dollars.
They had planned both the robbery and their _____ afterwards extremely carefully.

T7.5 Listen and check your answers. ☞ **p. 59**

Notice the different way that the verb and noun are stressed:

            ●   ●

verb: to break in   noun: a break-in

---

3 Mark the stress on the multi-word verbs and nouns in 2. Listen again and check your answers.
☞ **p. 59**

Practise saying the sentences with the correct stress.

8

The sounds /e/, /æ/, and /ʌ/
Pronunciation of the letters *e*, *a*, and *u*
Modal verbs in fast speech
Exaggeration and understatement
Stress in numbers

Sounds and spelling

1 The sounds /e/, /æ/, and /ʌ/

1 Work in pairs. Look at the following groups of three words. Use the pictures to help you understand the meaning of each word.

rebel   rabble   rubble

nets   gnats   nuts

trek   track   truck

flesh   flash   flush

2 **T8.1a** Listen to the tape. Circle the words you hear. Make sure you can hear the difference between them before you begin.

a rebel   rabble   rubble
b rebel   rabble   rubble
c rebel   rabble   rubble
d nets   gnats   nuts
e nets   gnats   nuts
f trek   track   truck
g trek   track   truck
h flesh   flash   flush
i flesh   flash   flush   p. 59

Practise making the sounds.

To make the sound /e/, open your mouth and smile. /e/ is a short sound.

Practise saying all the /e/ words in 1.

To make the sound /æ/, open your mouth more and don't smile so much. /æ/ is a short sound.

Practise saying all the /æ/ words in 1.

To make the sound /ʌ/, keep your mouth open but don't smile at all. /ʌ/ is a short sound.

Practise saying all the /ʌ/ words in 1.

---

3 Make a list of eight words in 1. Keep your list secret.

Now work in pairs.

Student A Say a word from your list.
Student B Point to the picture of it in 1.
Student A If your partner points to the correct picture, nod your head for 'Yes'. If your partner points to the wrong picture, shake your head for 'No'.

When you have finished, swap roles.

4 **T8.1b** Listen and write these words in the correct column below according to the sound of the underlined letters.

c<u>ou</u>rage	h<u>ea</u>vy	m<u>a</u>n	pl<u>ai</u>t	disc<u>u</u>ssion
l<u>ei</u>sure	<u>a</u>ny	s<u>ai</u>d	fri<u>e</u>nd	l<u>o</u>ve m<u>e</u>t

/e/	/æ/	/ʌ/

 p. 59

5 Write the shortest paragraph you can using all these words. Practise reading it aloud.

2 Pronunciation of the letters *e*, *a*, and *u*

1 **T8.2a** Listen to these groups of words. Circle the word in each group where the pronunciation of the letter *e* does not match the sound on the left.

a silent *e*   stor<u>ie</u>s   handsom<u>e</u>   l<u>e</u>ft   unmarri<u>e</u>d
b /ɪ/   pr<u>e</u>tty   mak<u>e</u>   haunt<u>e</u>d   hott<u>e</u>st
c /e/   succ<u>e</u>ss   w<u>e</u>dding   <u>e</u>xplanation   qui<u>e</u>t
d /iː/   g<u>e</u>nius   cath<u>e</u>dral   wom<u>e</u>n   m<u>e</u>dium
e /ə/   b<u>e</u>ing   cin<u>e</u>ma   poor<u>e</u>r   actr<u>e</u>ss

 p. 59

Listen again and practise saying the sounds and the matching words only.

2 **T8.2b** Listen to these different possible ways to pronounce the letter *a*.

/æ/	f<u>a</u>bulous	/e/	<u>a</u>nything
/eɪ/	rel<u>a</u>tions	/ə/	<u>a</u>gree
/ɑː/	d<u>a</u>nce	/ɒ/	sw<u>a</u>p
/ɪ/	vill<u>a</u>ge	silent *a*	marri<u>a</u>ge

T8.2c Listen to these pairs of words. Stop the tape at each tone. Complete the line with the correct example word above.

a <u>a</u>nswer, c<u>a</u>st, _____
b m<u>a</u>ny, <u>a</u>nybody, _____
c tragic<u>a</u>lly, carri<u>a</u>ge, _____
d b<u>a</u>sic, <u>a</u>ge, _____
e p<u>a</u>ssion, <u>a</u>ctor, _____
f wom<u>a</u>n, brilli<u>a</u>nt, _____
g cott<u>a</u>ge, lugg<u>a</u>ge, _____
h w<u>a</u>sp, y<u>a</u>cht, _____

 p. 59

3 Work in pairs. Think of other words spelt with *a* to match each sound. Check your answers in a dictionary. After five minutes compare your lists with other pairs. Which pair has got the longest list for each row?

4 **T8.2d** Listen to these surnames, which are all spelt with the letter *u*.

/ʌ/	/uː/	/juː/	/ʊ/	silent *u*
D<u>u</u>ff	L<u>u</u>cas	H<u>u</u>ghes	B<u>u</u>sh	G<u>u</u>est

Complete the sentences with the correct surname according to the pronunciation of the underlined letters.

a Ms _____ plays the g<u>u</u>itar.
b Mr _____ plays the fl<u>u</u>te.
c Ms _____ often goes b<u>u</u>ngee-j<u>u</u>mping.
d Ms _____ adores m<u>u</u>sicals.
e Mr _____ is a B<u>u</u>ddhist.
f Ms _____'s favourite season is s<u>u</u>mmer.
g Mr _____ loves p<u>u</u>ddings.
h Ms _____ loves bisc<u>u</u>its.
i Ms _____ wants to be a film prod<u>u</u>cer.
j Mr _____ is mad about parach<u>u</u>ting.

T8.2e Listen and check your answers.   p. 59

Listen again and repeat the sentences. Pay attention to the pronunciation of the letter *u*.

Connected speech and intonation

3 Modal verbs in fast speech

1 **T8.3a** Listen and complete these dialogues with the modal auxiliary verbs in the box.

can't   could   might   can't   may   must

a 'The boss isn't in today.'
  'No. I think she _____ <u>be</u> at a conference.'
b 'Has Sid put on some weight lately?'
  'No, he _____ <u>be</u> wearing a baggy suit, but I don't think he's put on any weight.'
c 'Has Erica left early?'
  'No, she _____ <u>have</u> gone home already. Her briefcase is still here.'

d 'Jon looks tired but pleased with himself this month.'
  'Yes. He _____ have been doing lots of overtime.'

e 'Where's this year's holiday rota?'
  'I'm not sure. Ms Armstrong in Accounts _____ have it.'

f 'Did you know that Derek's retiring next week?'
  'He _____ be! He looks so young!'

🔑 p. 59

2 What do you notice about the pronunciation of the underlined verbs *be* and *have* when they follow modal verbs?

3 Work in pairs. Read all the dialogues aloud, paying attention to the weak forms of *be* and *have*.

4 **T8.3b** Listen and respond with *must* or *can't*. Use the prompts below, like this:

a the office is empty.

| Is it lunch time? | **It must be lunch time – the office is empty.** | It must be lunch time – the office is empty. |

You listen   *You speak*   *You listen*

b she's just bought a new car.
c he looks a lot more confident.
d he's been on the phone for hours.
e she sounds so British.
f he's got a wedding ring.

🔑 p. 60

Modal auxiliary verbs can show degrees of probability:

She must be ill. (99% certain she's ill.)

She may be ill. (50% certain she's ill.)
    could
    might

She can't be ill. (99% certain she's not ill.)

We can also use intonation with *might* and *may* to show if these possibilities are unlikely or not.

---

5 **T8.3c** Listen to these sentences.

a She might be ill.
b She might be ill.
c He may be leaving.
d He may be leaving.

Which are unlikely possibilities? What is the intonation pattern in these sentences? What about the intonation in the others?

Listen again and check your answers.

🔑 p. 60

6 **T8.3d** Listen to these sentences. Mark the unlikely possibilities U.

a ☐ He might have resigned.
b ☐ She may have got promotion.
c ☐ We may be moving temporarily.
d ☐ They might be working late.
e ☐ He may be on a training course.
f ☐ He might be her new secretary.

🔑 p. 60

7 Work in pairs.
Student A Read a sentence from 6 aloud. Choose whether to use likely or unlikely intonation.
Student B Decide if the possibility is unlikely or not.

Intonation and sentence stress

4 Exaggeration and understatement

1 **T8.4** Listen to these dialogues. In each one you will hear two adjectives from the box. Copy them in the order you hear them.

annoyed	flabbergasted	parched
ravenous	thirsty	exhausted
furious	peckish	surprised
tired		

a _____ / _____
b _____ / _____
c _____ / _____
d _____ / _____
e _____ / _____

2 Who shows the strongest feelings in each dialogue? How do we know? How does the other person show their feelings? — p. 60

— p. 60

Notice the intonation for exaggeration.

I'm absolutely parched, aren't you?

Notice the intonation for understatement.

Well, I'm a bit thirsty.

---

3 Listen and repeat the dialogues, paying attention to intonation and stress.

4 Work with a partner. Make similar dialogues using the prompts below.

   a freezing/chilly
   b boiling/warm
   c devastated/upset
   d soaked/damp
   e terrified/scared

Word focus

5 Stress in numbers

It is often difficult to hear the difference between these numbers. Notice the different stress.

● thirty   ● thirteen

---

1 **T8.5a** Listen to these pairs of numbers and repeat them with the correct stress.

thirty   thirteen
forty   fourteen
fifty   fifteen
sixty   sixteen
seventy   seventeen
eighty   eighteen
ninety   nineteen

2 **T8.5b** Listen. What happens when you just list the *-teen* words? What happens when you say a *-teen* word as the first two digits in a date?

— p. 60

3 **T8.5c** Listen and circle the dates you hear.

   a She died in 1870/1817.
   b He was born in 1930/1913.
   c It began in 1450/1415.
   d The company was founded in 1980/1918.
   e They were married in 1540/1514.
   f It was published in 1790/1719.

The stress on thirty, forty, etc. doesn't vary.

● ● She was thirty when her first novel came out.

● ● She sells thirty thousand books a week.

The stress on thirteen, fourteen, etc. varies according to context.

● ● Eighteen million UK viewers saw the series.

● ● How many countries bought the series? Eighteen.

---

4 **T8.5d** Listen to these sentences and mark the main stress on the *-teen* words.

   a I paid thirteen dollars for it.
   b Emma's seventeen.
   c My jeans cost nineteen pounds.
   d Eighteen of my friends have a video camera.
   e She lives in Lindenstrasse, at number fifteen.
   f Twenty take away four is sixteen.

— p. 60

5 Circle the stress rules for *-teen* words.

---

a When a *-teen* word _is/is not_ followed by a noun, the *-teen* word is stressed ● ●.

b When a *-teen* word _is/is not_ followed by a noun, the *-teen* word is stressed ● ●.

The sounds /ð/, /d/, and /z/
The sounds /θ/, /ð/, /t/, /d/, /s/, and /z/
Polite intonation in indirect *wh-* questions
Antonyms

Sounds

1 The sounds /ð/, /d/, and /z/

1 **T9.1a** Listen to the first word on each of the cards below. Make sure that you can hear the difference between the sounds /ð/, /d/, and /z/.

/ð/

then	with	breathe
there	they	southern
loathe	those	clothing

/d/

den	dare	lied
sudden	day	she'd
tide	breed	load

/z/

Zen	whizz	she's
lies	lose	breeze
doze	closing	ties

2 **T9.1b** Listen and cross out the words you hear, like this:

You will hear each word twice.

Which card had the first row of crosses? Which was the last to have all the words crossed out?

Practise making the sounds.

You use your voice for all three sounds.

The sound /d/ is made further back in the mouth in English than in many languages.

If you have problems with the sound /ð/, try putting your finger in front of your mouth and touching it with your tongue, in the same way as the sound /θ/.

3 Work in groups of five or six. One person in each group is the caller. This person does not need to fill in the card below. The others should complete it with any nine words from 1.

The caller reads out the words from 1 in any order, and puts a cross (✘) next to each word as he reads (as a memory check). The others listen and cross out the words that they hear. The first person to cross out all the words shouts 'Bingo!'. Then the winner shows his / her card to check that the words on it are words that the caller has marked.

🔑 p. 60

2 The sounds /θ/, /ð/, /t/, /d/, /s/, and /z/

1 Read the dialogue. When you think the letters *th* are pronounced /θ/, underline them like this ___ . When you think the letters *th* are pronounced /ð/, underline them like this ∿∿∿ .

A How are Judith and Timothy Thorpe's triplets?

B Those three? Well … both Heather and Cathy are very healthy, but I think they're having rather a lot of trouble with Matthew.

A With Matthew? What's the matter with Matthew?

B Teething troubles, I think, and then he won't eat anything.

A Teething troubles? But how old are the triplets now?

B I think they're about thirteen months.

A Thirteen months? Oh, I thought they were a lot younger than that.

B No, they must be thirteen months because it was their first birthday at the end of last month – on the thirtieth … or was it the thirty-first?

A Oh dear, and I didn't send them anything, not even a birthday card … I wonder what Judith and Timothy thought?

B Don't distress yourself, dear, they didn't say anything to me …

2 **T9.2** Listen and check your answers.   **p. 61**

3 Listen again and repeat the dialogue in short sections.

Pay attention to your pronunciation of the sounds /θ/, /ð/, /t/, /d/, /s/, and /z/.

4 Practise reading the dialogue with a partner.

Stress and intonation

3 Polite intonation in indirect *wh*- questions

1 Look at the picture. Can you guess what question each person is asking? Put the words below in the correct order to form the questions, then match them to the people above.

a ☐ tell / how / me / could / photocopier/ the / works / you / ?

b ☐ happen / you / do / time / what / shuts / library / to / know / the/ ?

c ☐ is / you / the/ of / Jamaica / idea / capital / have / any / what / do / ?

d ☐ anyone / of / cup / I / a / can / know /get / coffee /does/ where / ?

e ☐ history / where / please / can / is / you / the /me / tell / section / ?

T9.3a Listen and check your answers.   **p. 61**

To make these questions sound polite, your voice starts high, comes down a lot, and goes up a little at the end like this:

Could you tell me how the photocopier works?

If you find this difficult, try humming the pattern like this:

mm mm MM mm MM mm MM mm mm mm MM ?

2 Listen again and practise the questions above, copying the stress and intonation on the tape.

3 Here are some more questions you might hear in the library. Put the words in the correct order.

a where / are / know / the / do / you / encyclopedias / ?

b photocopier / happen / where / I / get / the / can / to / you / for / change / know / do / ?

c which / can / borrow / I / tell / books / me / you / can / ?

d know / computer / how / anyone / works / this / does / ?

e keep / you / which / tell / could / newspapers / you / me / ?

f is / you / any / have / Georgia / where / idea / do / ?

g where / know / toilets / anyone / the / are / does / ?

T9.3b Listen and check your answers. Practise saying the questions, paying attention to the stress and intonation.

 p. 61

4 Think of some indirect questions to ask about your own classroom, school, library, etc. If possible, ask your teacher or the other students in your class.

Do you happen to know what time the reception desk closes?

Does anyone know if you can send e-mails from here?

Word focus

4 Antonyms

1 The antonym of a word is its opposite. We can use antonyms to agree with what someone has just said. Match the comments in the pictures and the box below to make dialogues in which the two speakers agree.

1 [f]   2 [ ]

3 [ ]   4 [ ]

5 [ ]   6 [ ]

a No, it's quite stressful, isn't it?

b Yes, it's not very encouraging, I agree.

c No, she can be very negative, can't she?

d Yes, it isn't terribly sensible, is it?

e I agree, I think it's completely unoriginal!

f It doesn't seem very likely, I must say.

T9.4a Listen and check your answers.   p. 61

2 Find the opposite pairs of adjectives in the dialogues in 1, then write them in the correct box below according to the stress patterns. If necessary, play the tape again to check your answers.

2 syllables

● ●	● ●
likely	

3 syllables

● ● ●	● ● ●
	unlikely

● ● ●

4 syllables

● ● ● ●	● ● ● ●

5 syllables

● ● ● ● ●	● ● ● ● ●

 p. 61

3 Write antonyms for these words. Either add a prefix, or use the words in the box below.

a successful _____
b useful _____
c complete _____
d consistent _____
e capable _____
f up-to-date _____
g superficial _____
h personal _____
i permanent _____
j significant _____
k practical _____
l normal _____
m realistic _____
n regular _____
o physical _____

out of date   temporary   profound   mental   useless

T9.4b Listen and check your answers. ◉━━ **p. 61**

4 Write the words in the correct column in 2 according to the stress pattern. Practise saying them. ◉━━ **p. 61**

5 **T9.4c** Listen and use antonyms to agree with the people on the tape, as in exercise 1. Speak during the pause on the tape, then listen to the correct answer.

I don't think his suggestion is practical.

I agree, it's completely impractical.

I agree, it's completely impractical.

You listen   *You speak*   *You listen*

10

The sounds /ʃ/, /tʃ/, and /dʒ/
Pronunciation of the letters *ch*
used to, *be / get used to*, and *usually* in fast speech
Stress
Rhyming words

Sounds and spelling

1 The sounds /ʃ/, /tʃ/, and /dʒ/

> /ʃ/ is the sound in *she*, *wash* and *precious*. To make the sound /ʃ/, open your lips a little, raise your tongue in the middle of your mouth, and breathe out. You should not use your voice.
>
> /tʃ/ is the sound in *change*, *kitchen*, and *watch*. To make the sound /tʃ/ you should start with the sound /t/ and then make the sound /ʃ/. You should not use your voice.
>
> /dʒ/ is the sound in *just*, *original*, and *large*. To make the sound /dʒ/ start with the sound /d/ and then make the sound /ʒ/, as in the word *television*. You should use your voice.

1 **T10.1a** Listen and tick (✔) the word you hear twice.

a   gin ☐   chin ☐   shin ☐

b   jeers ☐   cheers ☐   shears ☐

c   badge ☐   batch ☐   bash ☐

d   jaw ☐   chore ☐   shore ☐

e   marge ☐   march ☐   marsh ☐

f   jeep ☐   cheap ☐   sheep ☐

Check your answers.   🔑 p. 62

Listen again and practise saying the words.

2 **T10.1b** Work in groups of three. Each person chooses a card below. You will hear a word twice on the tape. If it is in the 'hear' column on your card, you begin. Say the word in the 'say' column next to the word you heard on tape. Continue in the same way. When another player says a word in the 'hear' column on your card, say the word next to it in the 'say' column.

A

You hear	You say
badge	cheers
sheep	march
chin	shears
batch	marge
jeers	gin
marsh	jeep

B

You hear	You say
shore	badge
cheers	shin
march	bash
jaw	batch
chore	jeers
gin	cheap

C

You hear	You say
jeep	shore
shin	sheep
bash	chin
shears	jaw
marge	chore
cheap	marsh

Who finishes saying the words on their card first? Who finishes last?

🔑 p. 62

2 Pronunciation of the letters *ch*

The letter combination *ch* has three main sound values, found in the following order of frequency:

a /tʃ/ as in *chip*

b /k/ as in *chemical*

c /ʃ/ as in *chef* (and other *ch* words of French origin)

1 Put these words into the correct columns. Which word has a silent *ch* and doesn't fit into any column?

bunches	character	echo	parachute
catch	charity	machine	pinch
chalet	children	mechanic	sachet
yacht	Christmas	moustache	school

/tʃ/	/k/	/ʃ/

T10.2 Listen and check your answers. 🔑 p. 62

Listen again and practise saying the words. Make sure you pronounce *ch* correctly each time.

Connected speech

3 *used to*, *be / get used to*, and *usually* in fast speech

1 Complete these foreign visitors' statements about living in Britain. Use either *used to*, *usually*, or a form of *be / get used to*.

a 'What's your favourite British drink?'
   'Well, I _____ drink tea here in Britain. It's better than British coffee.'

b 'Is there anything you find hard about life here?'
   'Well, I can't _____ the weather!'

c 'Have you found it easy to adapt to the British way of life?'
   'In general yes, but I still find driving a car here difficult. I suppose it's because I _____ driving on the right, not the left.'

d 'Was there anything you found strange about Britain before you came here?'
   'Yes. I _____ think double-decker buses were very strange before I came to London. But now I find them quite normal.'

e 'Did you find bacon and eggs for breakfast strange?'
   'Yes, but gradually I _____ it. I like the bacon now, but I still find fried egg a bit heavy first thing in the morning.'

f 'Have your tastes changed in other ways since coming to Britain?'
   'Yes, back at home I _____ drink warm beer, but now I drink it a lot and actually like it.'

T10.3a Listen and check your answers. 🔑 p. 62

Listen again and repeat the sentences. Make sure you pronounce *used to* /ˈjuːstə/ and *usually* /ˈjuːʒəli/ correctly.

2 Look at the picture of Sonia, a student from Italy. Complete her answers to these questions. Use either *used to*, *usually*, or a form of *be used to* or *get used to*. Remember that *be / get used to* needs an object. (*I'm used to it.*)

a What do you think about English spelling?

_____

_____

b Do you find American English difficult to understand?

_____

_____

c Do phonetic symbols look strange to you?

_____

_____

d How often do you work on your pronunciation in English classes?

_____

_____

> Italian spelling is very logical, so I get a shock every time I see an English word.

> My first English teacher came from Texas and I've always studied US English.

> At first phonetic symbols seemed like Martian but with each day I use them they're gradually becoming more ordinary – and so useful!

> We nearly always do a short pronunciation exercise in each of my English classes.

T10.3b Listen and check your answers. **p. 62**

3 Think about your language learning habits past and present. Write down some questions to ask a fellow student about their learning habits. When you have finished, interview each other in pairs.

Stress

4 Stress

1 Put these words into the correct columns according to the stress patterns.

amazing	destruction	magical
astonishing	discovery	radiation
dangerous	enjoyable	sympathetic
deceptive	godmother	telegram
defenceless	impossible	transformation

● ● ●	● ● ●	● ● ● ●	● ● ● ●
Superman	*depression*	*incredible*	*Cinderella*

T10.4a Listen and check your answers. **p. 62**

Listen again and repeat the words. Make sure you stress them correctly.

2 Sort out these lines to make two separate poems. (One is called 'Superman's Incredible Birthday Surprise' and the other is 'How the Fairy Godmother Cured Cinderella's Depression'.) Use the rhythm and rhymes as well as the sense to help you.

Write S by the lines from the 'Superman' poem. Write C by the lines from the 'Cinderella' poem.

> **Hello there, Superman,** *S*
> **Are you crying, Cinderella?** *C*
> **Don't be sorry,**
> **I've got a telegram**
> **Here's your chance:**
> **With my magic**
> **Wishing you Happy Returns of the day!**
> **And there's some kryptonite**
> **And your pumpkin**
> **Here in this parcel, so**
> **Now you're defenceless and can't run away.**
> **You will make it to the dance.**

The Red Knight
Sir Lancelot
Loved Guinevere
He blushed a lot
When she was near.

p. 62

Listen again and read the poems aloud. Make sure you stress them correctly and say them rhythmically.

Word focus

5 Rhyming words

1 Choose a word from the box which rhymes with each word below.

aisle	climb	laugh	quiet
aunt	debt	muscle	though
cheque	gnawed	quay	through

a rhyme *climb*   g who _____
b half _____   h plant _____
c sword _____   i rustle _____
d knee _____   j bet _____
e wreck _____   k smile _____
f know _____   l riot _____

T10.5a Listen and check your answers. p. 62

Listen again and repeat the words. Make sure you pronounce them correctly.

2 Fill the gaps in each sentence with a rhyming pair of words from 1.
  a The dragon *gnawed* Saint George's *sword* .
  b I gave my _____ a lovely _____ .
  c He signed a _____ to buy the _____ .
  d If you're in _____ , you shouldn't _____ .
  e I fell on the _____ and hurt my _____ .
  f We'll never _____ who wrote it, _____ .
  g Please be _____ and don't start a _____ !

T10.5b Listen and check your answers. p. 62

T10.4b Listen and check your answers. p. 62

Listen again and repeat the two poems. Make sure you stress them correctly and say them rhythmically.

3 T10.4c Listen to these poems and mark the stresses.

Bad boy makes good
•   •
Aladdin was lazy.
He never would learn.
But now he's a rich man
With money to burn.

11

The sounds /v/ and /w/, and silent *w*
The sounds /b/ and /v/, and silent *b*
Weak forms with past conditionals
Word linking in idiomatic expressions

Sounds and spelling

1 The sounds /v/ and /w/, and silent *w*

1 **T11.1a** Listen and circle the word you hear.

a veal wheel
b veils whales
c vine wine
d vest west
e viper wiper

🔑 **p. 63**

Practise saying the words above.

To make the sound /v/, your top teeth should touch the inside of your bottom lip.

To make the sound /w/, your teeth don't touch your lips. Your lips should be hard and round.

If you have problems with the sound /w/, try starting with /u:/ like this:

uuu: ➔ why
uu: ➔ why
u: ➔ why

2 **T11.1b** Listen to the conversation and fill in the boxes.

	1	2	3
A			
B			
C			

🔑 **p. 63**

3 Work in pairs. Without letting your partner see, write any nine /w/ and /v/ words in the grid marked *You*. Remember you can use a word more than once.

Student A Dictate what you have written.

Student B Write it in the grid marked *Your partner*.

When you have finished, swap roles.

You

	1	2	3
A			
B			
C			

Your partner

	1	2	3
A			
B			
C			

Example
A What's in box A1?
B West.
A And in box B1?
B Er … veal.

🔑 **p. 63**

4 Complete the crossword. All the words have a silent *w*.

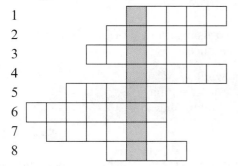

Clues
1 Two halves make a …
2 Ankle is to foot as … is to hand.
3 *Titanic* is a film about a very famous …
4 Long metal blade used as a weapon
5 Put words on paper.
6 A line on a face is called a …
7 Reply to a question
8 People often … a present up in coloured paper.

What is the word spelt out in the shaded column?

T11.1c Listen and repeat. Check your answers.
 p. 63

2 The sounds /b/ and /v/, and silent *b*

1 **T11.2a** Can you hear the difference between the sounds /b/ and /v/? Listen to these pairs of words. Write *1* next to the first word you hear and *2* next to the second word.

a ☐ ban   ☐ van
b ☐ best   ☐ vest
c ☐ bars   ☐ vase
d ☐ boats   ☐ votes
e ☐ bet   ☐ vet
f ☐ berry   ☐ very
g ☐ fibre   ☐ fiver
h ☐ dub   ☐ dove

 p. 63

Practise making the sounds.

To start the sound /b/, both lips should touch each other.

If you need to practise /v/, look at exercise 1.

---

2 Listen again and practise saying all the words in 1. Make sure that the difference between them is clear.

3 Write down six of the words in 1. Dictate them to a partner and then compare your lists.

4 **T11.2b** Here are some headlines from a sensational Sunday newspaper. Listen and then practise saying them. Pay attention to the pronunciation of /b/ and /v/.

British van driver banned from Costa Brava bar

Bomb victim Vivienne gives birth to baby boy

Brighton vicar leaves 'boring' wife for blonde barmaid

BRAVE BOB SAVES BABY VICKI FROM BLAZING BEDROOM

Violent Bolivian lover obsessed by vow of revenge

5 Cross out the silent *b*s in the words below.

lamb   climb   thumb   bombardment
numb   bomb   dumb   combination
comb   debt   crumb   number
limb   doubt   crumble   plumber
limbo   subtle   lumber   subtitle

T11.2c Listen and check your answers. **p. 63**

Practise saying the words with silent *b*.

Connected speech

3 Weak forms with past conditionals

1 **T11.3** Listen and write the number of words you hear in the boxes (*hadn't* = two words).

a [ ] _____ skidded if
   _____ icy.

b [ ] _____ faster,
   _____ killed.

c [ ] _____ afforded it
   _____ credit card.

d [ ] _____ searched _____
   _____ the jewels.

e [ ] _____ perfect
   _____ engine _____.

f [ ] _____ plane,
   _____ simpler.

g [ ] _____ crashed
   _____ braked suddenly.

h [ ] _____ to happen,
   _____ gone.

🔑 **p. 63**

2 Listen again and complete the sentences. 🔑 **p. 63**

3 How are these words pronounced when they come in the middle of sentences?

would have	wouldn't have
might have	might not have
could have	couldn't have

🔑 **p. 63**

Listen again and repeat the sentences, paying attention to the pronunciation of the words in the box.

4 Choose four of these sentences and put them into a story. You shouldn't change any of the words, and your story should be 80–100 words long. 🔑 **p. 63**

5 Read your story aloud.

4 Word linking in idiomatic expressions

1 The <u>underlined</u> parts of the sentences on page 49 can be replaced with the correct form of an idiom from the box below. Try to guess which.

to take something with a pinch of salt
to put your finger on it
to be like a red rag to a bull
to be on the tip of your tongue
to come to a sticky end
to not be yourself
to be at a loose end
to beat about the bush
to fly off the handle

a Don't mention politics to my father – you know <u>how it always makes him angry</u>!

_____

b Just say what you think – don't <u>avoid what you want to say because you feel embarrassed</u>. I believe in being direct with people.

_____

c At the end of the film the villain <u>had an unpleasant death, which he deserved</u>.

_____

d Yes, you're absolutely right! You've just <u>explained exactly something that a lot of people find difficult to understand</u>. I couldn't agree with you more!

_____

e I wish I could remember her name! <u>I can nearly remember it, but I just can't think of it</u> …

_____

f I'll help you if you like, <u>I've got nothing much to do</u>. Just call me when you need me!

_____

g Why do you <u>get suddenly angry</u> whenever I mention our financial problems? It really doesn't help.

_____

h What's up with Vince? He's <u>behaving strangely</u>.

_____

i What's Teresa been telling you about me? Whatever it is, <u>don't take it too seriously, because what she says is often untrue</u>.

_____

2 **T11.4a** Listen and write the exact phrases. Why might the idioms be difficult to understand on the tape?

🔑 p. 63

T11.4b Listen to the idioms again. Notice the different ways that words link together when we speak fast.

i(t)'s like a re(d) rag to͜ /w/ a bull

don'(t) beat͜ abou(t) the bush

he came to͜ /w/ a sticky͜ /j/ end

you've jus(t) pu(t) your finger͜ on͜ it

i(t)'s͜ on the tip͜ of my tongue

I'm͜ at͜ a loose end   you fly͜ /j/ off the handle

he's not (h)imself   take͜ it with͜ a pinch͜ of salt

Practise saying the idioms with the word linking shown.

---

3 Match the idioms in **A** to the meanings in **B**.

A

1 he's head over heels in love with her
2 at the eleventh hour
3 day in, day out
4 I've turned over a new leaf
5 he got out of the wrong side of bed
6 they don't see eye to eye
7 it cost the earth
8 he hit the roof

B

a every day, continuously
b they disagree or argue about something
c I've started behaving better
d he's madly in love with her
e it was extremely expensive
f he got extremely angry
g at the last possible moment
h he's been in a bad mood all day

4 Show which words link together in the idioms.

T11.4c Listen and check your answers. Practise saying the idioms.

🔑 p. 64

5 Work with a partner. Invent short dialogues using the idioms in 1 and 3 above.

Doesn't Mark realize what sort of a person Emma is?

You know what he's like – he won't listen to anything anyone tells him, and of course he's head over heels in love with

I suppose so.

Read the dialogues out to the class, paying attention to word linking.

12

Sound symbol crossword puzzle
Silent letter round-up
Assimilation
Emphatic forms
Homophones

Sounds and spelling

1 Sound symbol crossword puzzle

1 Use the clues in phonetic symbols and a dictionary to help you complete the crossword.

Crossword clues

1 Napoleon Bonaparte was a /smɔ:l/ man.
2 Madonna goes /'dʒɒgɪŋ/ regularly.
3 Greta Garbo had an amazing /feɪs/.
4 In Greek mythology the giant Atlas carried the sky on his /'ʃəʊldəz/.
5 Marie Curie's greatest /ə'tʃi:vmənt/ was the discovery of radium.
6 Auguste Rodin was a famous French /'skʌlptə/.
7 Quasimodo – the hero of Victor Hugo's book – had a hump on his /bæk/.
8 A giraffe has only seven bones in its /nek/.
9 Sir Christopher Wren /dɪ'zaɪnd/ Saint Paul's Cathedral.
10 Most countries in Western /'jʊərəp/ introduced a single currency – the Euro – in 1999.
11 Big Ben is a famous /klɒk/ tower in London.
12 'What a wonderful /wɜ:ld/' was sung by jazz musician Louis Armstrong.
13 The Bible and the Koran are two of the world's best-known /bʊks/.
14 The Taj Mahal is one of the most beautiful /'bɪldɪŋz/ in India.
15 Wolfgang Amadeus Mozart started composing when he was a young /bɔɪ/.
16 William Shakespeare was born in the /taʊn/ of Stratford-upon-Avon.
17 Oscar Wilde believed that all /ɑ:t/ was quite useless.
18 Hercules was a famous Greek /'hɪərəʊ/.
19 In Lewis Carroll's famous book, Alice had to go /θru:/ a rabbit hole to get into Wonderland.
20 Richard Wagner was for a time the /'prɒtəʒeɪ/ of mad King Ludwig of Bavaria.
21 The morning /ðət/ Princess Diana died BBC World Service radio stopped its normal broadcasts.
22 Malev is the Hungarian national /'eəlaɪn/.

2 Which famous artist's name is spelt out in the shaded column?

Check your answers. p. 64

2 Silent letter round-up

1 All these words contain letters which are not pronounced. Cross out the silent letters.

a han~~d~~ke~~r~~chief
b muscle
c Wednesday
d island
e sandwich
f leopard
g buoy
h corps
i Leicester
j handsome
k ironing
l bruise

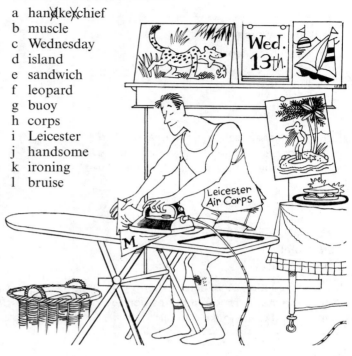

p. 64

T12.2a Listen and practise saying the words with the correct pronunciation. Keep the silent letters silent!

2 **T12.2b** Listen to some foreign students mispronouncing some of the words. Respond to what they say by echoing their words – but *not* their pronunciation.

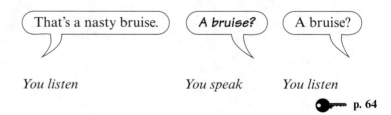

That's a nasty bruise.	*A bruise?*	A bruise?
You listen	*You speak*	*You listen*

p. 64

Connected speech

3 Assimilation

Look at these words:

American president
test blast
Washington graduate
old motel
target country

`T12.3a` In fast speech, the sound at the end of the first word is changed by the sound at the beginning of the second word. They sound like this:

America*m* president
tes*p* blast
Washingto*ng* graduate
ol*b* motel
targe*k* country

This is assimilation. Assimilation happens because the mouth moves into position for the second sound while making the first.

1 `T12.3b` Listen to these groups of words. <u>Underline</u> the sound that changes, and write what it changes to.

a whi<u>te</u> gloves
     k

   white coffee

   white paper

   white magic

   white bread

b red gold

   red carpet

   red pepper

   red medicine

   red-brick

c green grass

   green card

   green pepper

   Green movement

   green belt

 p. 64

Listen again and say the words fast, with assimilation. Look at the rules on page 64.

Intonation and sentence stress

4 Emphatic forms

In ordinary speech we often use contractions:
I'm fed up.
I've got a headache.
She'll be disappointed.

Sometimes, when we want to add emphasis, we use full forms instead of contractions.
*I **am** fed up!*
*I **have** got a headache!*
*She **will** be disappointed!*

Where there is no auxiliary verb, *do, does* or *did* add emphasis:
Have a drink.
***Do** have a drink!*
She has terrible taste in men.
*She **does** have terrible taste in men!*
She said some horrible things.
*She **did** say some horrible things!*

1 Write these sentences with extra emphasis.

a We won it. _____
b He gets on my nerves. _____
c I'm sorry. _____
d He promised me. _____
e They'll be pleased. _____
f I've missed you. _____
g You're being childish. _____
h Grow up. _____
i But I'd like to get into films.

   _____

j So where's Amy hiding? _____

 p. 64

`T12.4` Listen to these dialogues and check your answers. Each one ends with an emphatic form sentence.   p. 64

Listen again and practise saying the emphatic forms. Make sure you stress the auxiliary verbs.

Word focus

5 Homophones

Homophones are words which sound the same but which have a different spelling and a different meaning.

/tɪə/   tear   tier

1   There are two possible words for each phonetic transcription below. Can you find them?

a /sʌn/ *son* *sun*

b /feə/ _____ _____

c /beə/ _____ _____

d /swi:t/ _____ _____

e /raɪt/ _____ _____

f /əˈlaʊd/ _____ _____

p. 64

2   These sentences each contain one word which sounds correct but which is spelt wrongly. Underline these homophones and write the correct spelling.

a <u>Witch</u> channel is the film on? *Which*
b Who's watch is this? _____
c He used to be a kernel in the army. _____
d The dog wagged its tale happily. _____
e He isn't a town councillor, he's the mare of the town. _____
f The gorillas were armed with machine guns.

_____

g The lion gave a loud raw and then ran off.

_____

h The window's open and there's a terrible draft in here. _____

p. 64

Check the meaning of any new words in your dictionary.

Key

Unit 1

1 The sounds /iː/, /ɪ/, and /aɪ/

2 /aɪ/　　/ɪ/ /ɪ/
　　Icelandic fishermen
　　/ɪ/　　/aɪ/　/iː/
　　Italian ice-cream
　　/ɪ/　　　/aɪ//ɪ/
　　Indian spices
　　/ɪ/ /ɪ/　　　/ɪ/ /ɪ/
　　Egyptian linen
　　/aɪ//iː/　/ɪ/
　　Chinese silk
　　/iː//ɪ/　/ɪ/
　　Swedish films

2 The silent -e rule

Note: In English schools, children learn that silent -e makes the vowel before it 'say its name': a = /eɪ/, e = /iː/, i = /aɪ/, o = /əʊ/, u = /juː/.

1　**A** /ɪ/　/æ/　/ɒ/　/e/　/ʌ/
　　B /aɪ/　/eɪ/　/əʊ/　/iː/　/juː/

3　-ing　　　　　　-ed
　　spitting　　　　moped
　　winning　　　　whipped
　　coping　　　　noted
　　shopping　　　popped

　　-er　　　　　　-est
　　fitter　　　　　closest
　　cuter　　　　　thinnest
　　fatter　　　　　maddest
　　paler　　　　　saddest

3 Pronouns and verbs in fast speech

1　1 b　　2 c　　3 a

4　**T1.3b**
　　A Anyway, I suppose *you've* heard about Mark and Sonia?
　　B No, what?
　　A Oh, *didn't you* know? *They're* emigrating to New Zealand.
　　B Really, how come?
　　A I think *they've been* having a lot of problems lately – you knew their house *was* burgled last year, while *they were* asleep in bed?

B No, *I didn't* actually … how awful!
A Yeah, and Sonia*'s been* suffering with her nerves ever since, *she was* even off work for a while, I think.
B Oh no, I had no idea.
A And now apparently, Mark*'s been* made redundant from his job!
B The poor things!
A I know … so that's why *they've* decided to make a fresh start in New Zealand. I think Mark*'s being* paid quite a lot of redundancy money, so *they're* going to start up their own business.
B Oh … well I hope it works out for them. *Do you* know when *they're* leaving?
A *I don't* know but I think *they'll be* going before the end of the month.
B Oh, right – *I'll* give them a call to wish them all the best.
A Yes, *I'm* sure *they'd* appreciate that.

4 Hellos and goodbyes

2　1 *　　　3 **　　　5 **
　　2 ***　　4 ***　　6 *

5 Word families, stress, and the sound /ə/

3　**T1.5b**
industry
　　industrial
　　　　industrialist
invention　　　　industrialize
　　inventive
　　　　inventor
competition　　　invent
　　competitive
　　　　competitor
criticism　　　　compete
　　critical
　　　critic
　　　　criticize

politics
　　political
　　　　politician
nation　　　　politicize
　　nationalistic
　　　　nationalist
analysis　　　　nationalize
　　analytical
　　　　analyst
　　　　analyse

Unit 2

1 The sound /h/ and linking /w/ and /j/

1　**T2.1a**
　　a What nice clean *air*!
　　b Will you *eat* that soup up?
　　c There's something wrong with my *hearing*!
　　d Do you like *eels*?

4　a Henry and I agree you are to inherit the antique hatstand.
　　b Helen was free at seven, and she hurried to meet Joe at the opera house.
　　c Holly admires my nephew Hugh a lot. He's a handsome boy, and so intelligent too.

2 Silent letter *h*

1　a *hotel* – in modern English the *h* is sounded in *hotel*. In the other words it is silent.
　　b *perhaps* – the *h* is sounded and the *r* is silent in *perhaps* in standard British English. In the other words the *r* is sounded and the *h* is silent.
　　c *whole* – the *h* is sounded and the *w* is silent in *whole*. In the other words the *w* is sounded and the *h* is silent. In England, initial *wh*- is usually pronounced /w/ these days. In Scotland it is still sometimes pronounced /hw/, eg /hweɪl/, /hwen/, /hwaɪt/.

2 a heir, honest, hours
  b /r/ c /w/, /h/

3 yog**h**urt   ex**h**austed
  ex**h**ibition   **h**eirloom
  ve**h**icle   g**h**astly
  heritage   harmony
  prehistoric   hostel
  hospital   diarr**h**oea

3 Strong and weak forms of prepositions

3 a strong b weak

4 Exclamations

1 ▮ T2.4a
  a hideous   attractive
  b disgusting   delicious
  c sensible   foolish
  d stale   fresh
  e smart   shabby
  f gorgeous   ghastly
  g cheerful   depressing
  h varied   monotonous

2 a advice   suggestion
  b bread   loaf
  c clothes   outfit
  d food   meal
  e luggage   case
  f music   tune
  g weather   climate
  h work   job

3 b What a shabby suitcase!
  c What a gorgeous climate!

5 ▮ T2.4c
  A delicious meal
  B What a delicious meal!

  A stale bread
  B What stale bread!

  A varied job
  B What a varied job!

  A depressing music
  B What depressing music!

  A ghastly weather
  B What ghastly weather!

  A smart hotel
  B What a smart hotel!

  A foolish advice
  B What foolish advice!

  A attractive outfit
  B What an attractive outfit!

5 Stress in phrasal verbs

1 a She put on her shoes.

  b She put her shoes on.

  c She put them on.

2 a take back   d take in
  b put off   e put up
  c put together   f put out

3 ▮ T2.5b
  A He's put our meeting off.
  B He's put it off.

  A She took off her sunglasses.
  B She took them off.

  A I can't put together that clock kit.
  B I can't put it together.

  A They've put up interest rates.
  B They've put them up.

  A We took back those faulty headphones.
  B We took them back.

  A I can't take in what she's saying.
  B I can't take it in.

  A Put that light out!
  B Put it out!

Unit 3

1 The sound /r/ in British and American English

1 | | British | American |
|---|---|---|
| b | ✔ reliable | ✔ reliable |
| c | ✔ practical | ✔ practical |
| d | ✘ sincere | ✔ sincere |
| e | ✘ organized | ✔ organized |
| f | ✔ proud | ✔ proud |
| g | ✔ relaxed | ✔ relaxed |
| h | ✘ careless | ✔ careless |
| i | ✘ popular | ✔ popular |

2 a When r comes before a vowel sound, it is pronounced in both US and GB English.

  b When r comes after a vowel sound, it is pronounced in US English, but not in GB English.

4 The r at the end of over- is pronounced when the word (or syllable) that follows begins with a vowel. It is not pronounced when the word (or syllable) afterwards begins with a consonant sound.

5 The meaning of over- is 'more … than necessary'.
  Sample answers:
  over-modest: She prepared all the food for the party herself, but she doesn't want anyone to know.
  over-qualified: He's passed lots of exams but is applying for a job as a roadsweeper.
  over-confident: He thinks he can climb Mount Everest after one climbing lesson.
  overpaid: The Accounts department made a mistake and this month she was paid double.
  over-educated: He's studied at university for many years and now he can't find a job that he'll accept.
  over-excited: The children were far too excited to sleep on Christmas Eve.
  over-ambitious: He wants to be an actor, an astronaut, and an artist all at the same time.

6 **Laura** Matthew! Are you going anywhere over Easter this year?
  Matthew Well, yes, as a matter of fact, we are. We're off on a tour of Italy for a week or two.
  Laura Mmm. That sounds great! Where exactly will you be going?
  Matthew Oh, here and there. Rome's more or less definite, but we're open to suggestions.
  Laura Are you travelling by coach?
  Matthew No, by car actually.
  Laura When you're in Rome, you must throw a coin over your shoulder into the Trevi fountain.
  Matthew Really? What for?
  Laura It means, sooner or later, you're sure to return.

2 Linking with book and film titles

2 The Mayor of Casterbridge
Pride and Prejudice
Alice in Wonderland
Jane Eyre
Great Expectations
The Hound of the Baskervilles

3 Rising and falling intonation in questions

1 **T3.3a**

A So you've applied for a job as a holiday rep and you'd like to work in Greece?
B Yes, that's right.
A Why Greece?
B I've been there on holiday, and I just sort of thought it would be a nice place to work for the summer … you know, quite relaxing …
A Hmmm … and do you speak Greek?
B Erm, a bit … my Greek boyfriend last year taught me quite a few useful phrases …
A Hmmm … It might be rather difficult if you don't speak Greek … . Do you speak any other languages at all?
B I speak French quite fluently, and quite a bit of Spanish …
A Aha … so how did you learn French?
B Well at school mostly … and I went on holiday to France a lot when I was a child …
A Hmmm … and which other languages did you say you speak?
B Just Spanish …
A Do you speak Spanish well?
B Well, not as well as French …
A Hmmm … Okay, well let's move on. What about previous work experience? I see from your application form … you spent two summers working on a farm?
B Yes, my uncle's a farmer, so I was helping him, looking after the animals and so on …
A Hmmm, very nice, I'm sure … not much help for working as a holiday rep though, is it? What other jobs have you done?

B I worked part-time in a clothes shop when I was at school, and last summer I had a job as a waitress … in a casino …
A In a casino? Are you old enough to work in a casino?
B Yes, I'm twenty-two actually.
A Hmm, yes, well I think that's everything … we'll be in touch.

a 5 b 9 c 8 d 1 e 12 f 4 g 11 h 6
i 2 j 7 k 10 13

2 **T3.3b**

And you'd like to work in Greece? ↗
Why Greece? ↘
Do you speak Greek? ↗
Do you speak any other languages at all? ↗
So how did you learn French? ↘
Which other languages did you say you speak? ↗
Do you speak Spanish well? ↗
What about previous work experience? ↘
You spent two summers working on a farm? ↗
What other jobs have you done? ↘
In a casino? ↗
Are you old enough to work in a casino? ↗

4 Stress in compound adjectives

1, 2 **T3.4a**

a left-handed
b self-centred
c badly-dressed
d well-behaved
e quick-tempered
f overweight
g broad-minded
h good-looking

3 1 e 2 c 3 d 4 a 5 b 6 h 7 f 8 g

5 Opposites with dis-, il-, im-, in-, ir-, and un-

1 a dishonest i illogical
  b unreliable j immoral
  c impolite k incorrect
  d irrational l unreasonable
  e immature m irresponsible
  f informal n unacceptable
  g illegal o impossible
  h dissatisfied

2 a We often use im- with words beginning with the letters p or m.
  b We often use il- with words beginning with the letter l.
  c We often use ir- with words beginning with the letter r.

3 **T3.5a**

• • • _____	• • ● _____
dishonest	impolite
informal	immature
illegal	incorrect
immoral	

• • ● • • _____	• ● • • _____
unreliable	irrational
irresponsible	dissatisfied
unacceptable	illogical
	unreasonable
	impossible

Unit 4

1 The sounds /əʊ/, /ɔː/, and /ɒ/

2 **T4.1b**

on the boat	at the airport	on the lorry
/əʊ/	/ɔː/	/ɒ/
bowls	corn	cloth
tomatoes	strawberries	coffee
cocoa	footballs	olive oil
tobacco		pottery
gold		sausages
clothes		soft
precious stones		drinks

The boat has the longest list.
The airport has the shortest.

2 Pronunciation of the letter *o*

1 a both /əʊ/   d done /ʌ/
   b women /ɪ/   e whole /əʊ/
   c polish /ɒ/

2 a ✗   c ✗   e ✔
   b ✔   d ✗   f ✗

3 Sentences with and without the indefinite article

1 b, c, f, g, i, l

3 1 b   5 c   9 i
   2 k   6 f   10 l
   3 g   7 a   11 d
   4 j   8 h   12 e

4 *Wh-* questions with up intonation

2 a Last Monday.
   b I was unemployed.
   c One or two.
   d Just a short time.
   e From a friend.
   f Selling make-up.

5 Homographs

1 T4.5b
   a Why do teenagers rebel against their parents? **2**
   b Can you sign this contract please? **1**
   c Today rebel forces attacked the capital. **1**
   d Blood vessels contract in cold weather. **2**
   e James Dean was a 1950s rebel. **1**
   f Our firm specializes in contract law. **1**

2 a nouns
   b verbs

3 a 2   d 3   g 8
   b 1   e 5   h 7
   c 4   f 6

Unit 5

1 'Dark' /l/ and 'clear' /l/

1 a *2, 1*   d *2, 1*
   b *1, 2*   e *2, 1*
   c *1, 2*

---

3 T5.1c
   a leaf   feel   e lick   kill
   b less   sell   f lip   pill
   c lit   till   g light   tile
   d lean   kneel   h let   tell

2 Silent *l*

1 a half   e cold
   b walk   f would
   c calm   g shoulder
   d folk

3 a calf, on behalf of …
   b stalk, chalk
   c palm, psalm
   d yolk
   e bold, fold
   f could, should
   g boulder, mould

3 Linking with *and* in common phrases

1 T5.3a
   a Come and look what I've found!
   b 'Do you still want to change jobs?'
      'I've decided to wait and see what happens.'
   c 'Can you give me a refund for this, please?'
      'I'll just go and ask the manager if that's OK.'
   d 'I've got so much to do this afternoon!'
      'I'll try and help you when I've finished this.'
   e 'Thanks – we've had a lovely time!'
      'You must come and see us again soon.'
   f I'll just go and post this letter.
   g I think I'll try and phone a taxi.

4 a pros and cons
   b in and out
   c More and more
   d up and down
   e odds and ends
   f better and better
   g on and on
   h worse and worse
   i backwards and forwards
   j now and again

---

4 Special stress

1 a 'Have Ben and Ellen gone home?'
      'Ben has, but I think Ellen's still here.'
   b 'I'm sorry I can't go shopping with you this afternoon – I've still got a lot of work to do.'
      'You could go if you wanted to!'
   c 'What's the matter? You look really fed up.'
      'I'm just so annoyed with Philip, you'll never guess what he's done now.'
   d 'Is this your coat?'
      'No, that one's mine.'

2 disagree *b*   contradict *d*
   contrast *a*   emphasize *c*

3 a It said $4 on the sign over there!
   b I do, and the children do, but my husband doesn't very much, he gets bored.
   c It was hilarious, wasn't it? We were killing ourselves with laughing!
   d You might, if you did a bit of studying.
   e Not again! I only changed it last week!
   f Thirty-five, unfortunately!
   g I will finish it, honestly, Mum … later …
   h Thank you for coming!

5 Words ending in *-ion*

2 The stress is on the next to last syllable. *-ion* is pronounced /ən/.

3

	short	long
a	/æ/	/eɪ/
	fashion	occupation communication
e	/e/	/iː/
	profession question	completion
o	/ɒ/	/əʊ/
	option	promotion emotion
u	/ʌ/	/uː/
	instruction	solution conclusion

4 If there is one consonant between the stressed syllable and the *-ion* suffix, then the vowel sound is long.
If there are two or more consonants between the stressed syllable and the *-ion* suffix, then the vowel sound is short.

Unit 6

1 The sound /ŋ/ (and /n/, /ŋg/, /ŋk/, and /ndʒ/)

1 `T6.1b`

a thing   c pink   e bang
b win   d sink   f banner

4,5 `T6.1d`

a Aunt Angela banged her ankle while dancing a <u>tango</u> with Uncle Frank at a Birmingham skating-rink.
b The Hong Kong banker drinking gin in a <u>singles'</u> bar winked at the pretty young woman who was singing romantic songs.
c What's that incredibly long pink stringy thing on <u>Angus</u> King's tongue?

6 `T6.1e`

/ŋə/	/ŋgə/	/ndʒə/
singer	anger	stranger
hanger	finger	danger
banger	stronger	challenger
	longer	plunger
		ginger

2 Silent letters *g*, *k*, and *n*

1 a signature   c autumnal
   b banknote

2 a When the letters *gn* come at the beginning or the end of a word – but not the middle – *g* is silent.
b When the letter *k* comes before the letter *n* at the beginning of a word, *k* is silent.
c When the letter *n* comes after the letter *m* at the end of a word, *n* is silent.

3 a kneel   d column
   b autumn   e knowledge
   c foreign   f sign

3 Unpronounced /d/, /b/, /g/, /t/, /p/, and /k/

3 a Rose is our younges~~t~~ daughter.
b She's wearing a re~~d~~ T-shirt.
c It's a bi~~g~~ computer company.
d His alarm cloc~~k~~ goes off at eight.
e I love ri~~pe~~ bananas!
f What are my jo~~b~~ prospects?

4 Sentence phrasing

1 `T6.4b`

1 a I got a card from my aunt, who lives in Paris.
b I got a card from my aunt who lives in Paris.
2 a The computer, which we bought in July, was stolen.
b The computer which we bought in July was stolen.
3 a The UK car plant employees who protested lost their jobs.
b The UK car plant employees, who protested, lost their jobs.
4 a Jason wanted to prepare a meal which was unusual.
b Jason wanted to prepare a meal, which was unusual.

2 1 a I have only one aunt. I got a card from her. She lives in Paris.
b I have more than one aunt. I got a card from the one living in Paris.
2 a We have only one computer. We bought it in July. It was stolen.
b We have more than one computer. One of our computers was stolen – the one we bought in July.
3 a Some of the UK car plant employees protested. Those people lost their jobs.
b All the UK car plant employees protested. All lost their jobs.
4 a Jason wanted to prepare an unusual meal.
b Jason wanted to prepare a meal. This fact was unusual.

5 *-ed* adjectives + /d/, /t/, /ɪd/ (and exceptions)

1 a Boy: 'I'm bored.'
   Teacher: 'I'm worried.'
b Boy: 'She's disgusted.'
   Teacher: 'I'm disappointed.'
c Boy: 'I'm embarrassed.'
   Parents: 'We're shocked.'

2
/d/	/t/	/ɪd/
bored	shocked	disappointed
worried	embarrassed	disgusted

3 a When *-ed* follows the sound /d/ or /t/, it is pronounced /ɪd/.
b When *-ed* follows a voiceless consonant sound apart from /t/, it is pronounced /t/.
c When *-ed* follows a vowel sound, or a voiced consonant apart from /d/, it is pronounced /d/.

4 `T6.5b`

a wicked   d rugged
b ragged   e beloved
c naked   f jagged

Unit 7

1 The sounds /θ/, /s/, and /t/

2 `T7.1b`

a tie thigh sigh thigh
b sick tick thick tick
c theme team seem team
d path path pass part
e tent tense tenth tense
f force fourth force fought

2 Pronunciation of *s*

1 `T7.2b`

a /ʒ/   b /z/   c /s/   d /ʒ/   e /s/

2 a /ʒ/   b /z/   c /s/   d /ʒ/   e /s/

3 a expansion, extension /ʃ/
b dose /s/
c disease, tease /z/
d insure /ʃ/
e disaster /z/

-sion is pronounced /ʒn/ after vowels (e.g. confu<u>sion</u>), but /ʃn/ after consonants (e.g. expan<u>sion</u>).
-ose is usually pronounced /əʊz/. Exceptions: close *(adv/adj)* /kləʊs/, dose /dəʊs/.

-ease is sometimes pronounced /iːs/ (e.g. grease), and sometimes /iːz/ (e.g. please). You have to learn each word separately.

-sure is usually pronounced /ʒə/, but it can be pronounced /ʃɔː/ (eg insure, ensure, assure) or /ʃə/ (eg pressure). You have to learn each word separately.

dis- is always pronounced /dɪs/ when it is a prefix that means 'the opposite of' (e.g. dishonest). In words where it is not a prefix, *dis-* is sometimes pronounced /dɪz/ (e.g. disease /dɪˈziːz/ and disaster /dɪˈzɑːstə/).

3 Linking phrases with *get*

1 `T7.3a`

a 'Hurry up and get ready, or you'll miss the bus!'
'Good, I hate school!'
b 'Why is it we always get lost when you drive?'
'Because you can't read the map.'
c 'Do you like your new job then?'
'I didn't much at first, but I've got used to it now.'
d 'You're late!'
'Sorry, I just couldn't get away from the office.'
e 'Get in touch with me as soon as you get there, won't you?'
'Yeah, sure.'
f 'I'll go and get everyone a drink, shall I? What do you want?'
'I think I'll have a beer, please.'

4 Stress in compounds with nouns and adjectives

1, 2 `T7.4a`

a a mobile phone
b corkscrew
c personal stereo
d vacuum cleaner
e tin opener
f portable TV
g electric kettle
h answering machine

3 a headphones
b computer game
c coffee maker
d electric razor
e dishwasher
f washing machine
g digital television
h central heating
i CD player
j video recorder
k fan heater

5 Stress in multi-word verbs and nouns

1 a a get-together
b a lookout
c a breakdown
d a getaway
e a take-off
f a sell-out
g a round-up

2, 3 `T7.5`

b Look out … lookout
c sell-out … sold out
d get together … get-together
e take-off … taking off
f rounds up … round-up
g got away … getaway

Unit 8

1 The sounds /e/, /æ/, and /ʌ/

2 `T8.1a`

a rabble	d nets	g truck
b rebel	e gnats	h flush
c rubble	f trek	i flash

4 `T8.1b`

/e/	/æ/	/ʌ/
heavy	man	courage
leisure	plait	discussion
any		love
said		
friend		
met		

2 Pronunciation of the letters *e*, *a*, and *u*

1 a left /e/   d women /ɪ/
b make /eɪ/   e being /iː/
c quiet /ə/

2 a dance   e fabulous
b anything   f agree
c marriage   g village
d relations   h swap

4 `T8.2e`

a Ms Guest plays the guitar.
b Mr Lucas plays the flute.
c Ms Duff often goes bungee-jumping.
d Ms Hughes adores musicals.
e Mr Bush is a Buddhist.
f Ms Duff's favourite season is summer.
g Mr Bush loves puddings.
h Ms Guest loves biscuits.
i Ms Hughes wants to be a film producer.
j Mr Lucas is mad about parachuting.

3 Modal verbs in fast speech

1 `T8.3a`

a 'The boss isn't in today.'
'No. I think she may be at a conference.'
b 'Has Sid put on some weight lately?'
'No, he might be wearing a baggy suit, but I don't think he's put on any weight.'
c 'Has Erica left early?'
'No, she can't have gone home already. Her briefcase is still here.'
d 'Jon looks tired but pleased with himself this month.'
'Yes. He must have been doing lots of overtime.'
e 'Where's this year's holiday rota?'
'I'm not sure. Ms Armstrong in Accounts could have it.'
f 'Did you know that Derek's retiring next week?'
'He can't be! He looks so young!'

2 When the auxiliary verb *have* follows a modal verb, it is pronounced /əv/:
can't have = /ˈkɑːntəv/
must have = /ˈmʌstəv/

When *have* as a main verb follows a modal verb (as in dialogue e) it is pronounced /hæv/.

When *be* follows a modal verb, it is pronounced /bɪ/ (been = /bɪn/):
might be = /ˈmaɪpbɪ/
can't be = /ˈkɑːmpbɪ/
must have been = /ˈmʌstəvbɪn/

4 **T8.3b**
a A Is it lunch time?
  B It must be lunch time – the office is empty.
b A Does Donna have financial problems?
  B She can't have financial problems – She's just bought a new car.
c A Has Carl been on a management course?
  B He must have been on a management course – he looks a lot more confident.
d A Is Gerry speaking to his girlfriend?
  B He must be speaking to his girlfriend – he's been on the phone for hours.
e A Is Gwyn American?
  B She can't be American – she sounds so British.
f A Is Kieran single?
  B He can't be single – he's got a wedding ring.

5 Sentences a and c are unlikely possibilities. The intonation pattern in these sentences is like this:

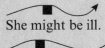

She might be ill.

He may be leaving.

The intonation pattern in the other sentences is like this:

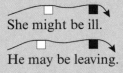

She might be ill.

He may be leaving.

6 a U   c U   e –
  b –   d –   f U

4 **Exaggeration and understatement**

1 **T8.4**
a A I'm absolutely *parched*, aren't you?
  B Well, I'm a bit *thirsty*, I must admit.
b A I'm absolutely *ravenous*, aren't you?
  B Well, I'm a little *peckish*.
c A I'm totally *exhausted*, aren't you?
  B Well, I'm quite *tired*.
d A I'm completely *flabbergasted*, aren't you?
  B Well, I'm a little *surprised*.
e A I'm utterly *furious*, aren't you?
  B Well, I'm a bit *annoyed*.

2 Speaker 1 shows strong feelings by:
• choosing a very strong adjective
• using an extreme modifier (absolutely, utterly, totally, completely)
• using intonation which is very emphatic – starting very high and falling dramatically on the modifier and the adjective. (This is known as high fall intonation.)

Speaker 2 shows measured feelings by:
• choosing a less strong adjective
• using a moderate modifier (quite, a bit, a little)
• using intonation which shows reservation – rising on the modifier, falling on the adjective, and rising at the end of the sentence. (This is known as fall-rise intonation.)

5 **Stress in numbers: 30 / 13 (with dates)**

2 **T8.5b**
When you just list the *-teen* words the stress shifts to the first part of each word – the bit that is different: '<u>thir</u>teen, <u>four</u>teen, <u>fif</u>teen, <u>six</u>teen, <u>seven</u>teen, <u>eigh</u>teen, <u>nine</u>teen…'.

When you say a *-teen* word as the first two digits of a date, the stress also shifts to the first part of the word: '<u>seven</u>teen seventy-five'.

3 a 1870   d 1918
  b 1930   e 1540
  c 1415   f 1719

4 a thirtéen
  b seventéen
  c ninetéen
  d eightéen
  e fiftéen.
  f sixtéen

5 a When a *-teen* word is followed by a noun, the *-teen* word is stressed ● •.
  b When a *-teen* word is not followed by a noun, the *-teen* word is stressed •●.

Unit 9

1 The sounds /ð/, /d/, and /z/

2 **T9.1b**
Zen dare breeze clothing loathe ties doze lies day there she's southern closing tide breathe those whizz load lied den she'd they lose with sudden then breed

The /z/ card had the first row of crosses.
The /d/ card was the last to have all the words crossed out.

2 The sounds /θ/, /ð/, /t/, /d/, /s/, and /z/

1 A How are Judith and Timothy Thorpe's triplets?
  B Those three? Well … both Heather and Cathy are very healthy, but I think they're having rather a lot of trouble with Matthew.
  A With Matthew? What's the matter with Matthew?
  B Teething troubles, I think, and then he won't eat anything.

A Teething troubles? But how old are the triplets now?

B I think they're about thirteen months.

A Thirteen months? Oh, I thought they were a lot younger than that.

B No, they must be thirteen months because it was their first birthday at the end of last month – on the thirtieth … or was it the thirty-first?

A Oh dear, and I didn't send them anything, not even a birthday card … I wonder what Judith and Timothy thought?

B Don't distress yourself, dear, they didn't say anything to me …

3 Polite intonation in indirect *wh-* questions

1 **T9.3a**

a Could you tell me how the photocopier works? **4**

b Do you happen to know what time the library shuts? **5**

c Do you have any idea what the capital of Jamaica is? **1**

d Does anyone know where I can get a cup of coffee? **2**

e Can you tell me where the history section is, please? **3**

3 **T9.3b**

a Do you know where the encyclopedias are?

b Do you happen to know where I can get change for the photocopier?

c Can you tell me which books I can borrow?

d Does anyone know how this computer works?

e Could you tell me which newspapers you keep?

f Do you have any idea where Georgia is?

g Does anyone know where the toilets are?

4 Antonyms

1 **T9.4a**

1 **A** I think a thunderstorm's very unlikely, don't you?

  B It doesn't seem very likely, I must say.

2 **A** What Tony wants to do is ridiculous!

  B Yes, it isn't terribly sensible, is it?

3 **A** I have to say, I don't think his new book is very original!

  B I agree, I think it's completely unoriginal!

4 **A** This month's sales forecast is a bit disappointing, don't you think?

  B Yes, it's not very encouraging, I agree.

5 **A** I'm not finding this evening very relaxing, are you?

  B No, it's quite stressful, isn't it?

6 **A** Her attitude's not very positive sometimes!

  B No, she can be very negative, can't she?

2 ●•

likely
stressful

●••	•●•
sensible	unlikely
positive	relaxing
negative

•●••	••●•
ridiculous	disappointing
original	encouraging

••●••

unoriginal

3 **T9.4b**

a unsuccessful
b useless
c incomplete
d inconsistent
e incapable
f out of date
g profound
h impersonal
i temporary
j insignificant
k impractical
l abnormal
m unrealistic
n irregular
o mental

4 ●•	•●
useful	complete
useless	profound
normal
mental

●••	•●•
capable	successful
personal	consistent
permanent	abnormal
temporary
practical
regular
physical

| ••●
---|---
| incomplete
| up-to-date
| out of date

•●••	••●•
incapable	unsuccessful
impersonal	inconsistent
significant	superficial
impractical	realistic
irregular

••●••	•••●•
insignificant	unrealistic

5 **T9.4c**

a **A** I don't think his suggestion is practical.

  B I agree, it's completely impractical.

b **A** The amount John works is abnormal.

  B I agree, it isn't normal, is it?

c **A** The budget we've been given is completely unrealistic.

  B I agree, it isn't very realistic, is it?

d **A** That lecture on Friday was useless!

  B I agree, it wasn't very useful, was it?

e **A** I though the whole film was very superficial.

  B I agree, it wasn't very profound, was it.

f **A** Most of the equipment in this school is completely out of date!

  B I agree, it isn't very up-to-date, is it?

g **A** I thought the meeting was completely unsuccessful.

  B I agree, it wasn't very successful, was it?

Unit 10

1 The sounds /ʃ/, /tʃ/, and /dʒ/

1 **T10.1a**

a gin chin chin shin
b jeers cheers shears shears
c badge batch bash badge
d jaw shore chore shore
e marge march marsh march
f jeep cheap sheep jeep

2 **T10.1b**

jeep ... jeep

B finishes saying the words first.
A finishes last.

2 Pronunciation of the letters *ch*

1 **T10.2**

/tʃ/	/k/	/ʃ/
bunches	character	chalet
catch	Christmas	machine
charity	echo	moustache
children	mechanic	parachute
pinch	school	sachet

yacht /jɒt/ has a silent *ch* and doesn't fit into any column.

3 *used to*, *be / get used to*, and *usually* in fast speech

1 **T10.3a**

a 'What's your favourite British drink?'
'Well, I usually drink tea here in Britain. It's better than British coffee.'
b 'Is there anything you find hard about life here?'
'Well, I can't get used to the weather!'
c 'Have you found it easy to adapt to the British way of life?'
'In general yes, but I still find driving a car here difficult. I suppose it's because I'm used to driving on the right, not the left.'
d 'Was there anything you found strange about Britain before you came here?'
'Yes. I used to think double-decker buses were very strange before I came to London. But now I find them quite normal.'
e 'Did you find bacon and eggs for breakfast strange?'
'Yes, but gradually I'm getting used to it. I like the bacon now, but I still find fried egg a bit heavy first thing in the morning.'
f 'Have your tastes changed in other ways since coming to Britain?'
'Yes, back at home I didn't use to drink warm beer, but now I drink it a lot and actually like it.'

2 **T10.3b**

a I can't get used to it.
b No. I'm used to it.
c Well, I'm getting used to them.
d I usually work on my pronunciation in each of my English classes.

4 Stress

1 **T10.4a**

●●●	●●●
Superman	depression
dangerous	amazing
godmother	deceptive
magical	defenceless
telegram	destruction

●●●●	●●●●
incredible	Cinderella
astonishing	radiation
discovery	sympathetic
enjoyable	transformation
impossible	

2 **T10.4b**

Superman's Incredible Birthday Surprise
Hello there, Superman,
I've got a telegram
Wishing you Happy Returns of the day!
And there's some kryptonite
Here in this parcel, so
Now you're defenceless and can't run away.

How the Fairy Godmother Cured Cinderella's Depression
Are you crying, Cinderella?
Don't be sorry,
Here's your chance:
With my magic
And your pumpkin
You will make it to the dance.

3 **Bad boy makes good**
Aladdin was lazy.
He never would learn.
But now he's a rich man
With money to burn.

The Red Knight
Sir Lancelot
Loved Guinevere
He blushed a lot
When she was near.

5 Rhyming words

1 **T10.5a**

a	rhyme	climb
b	half	laugh
c	sword	gnawed
d	knee	quay
e	wreck	cheque
f	know	though
g	who	through
h	plant	aunt
i	rustle	muscle
j	bet	debt
k	smile	aisle
l	riot	quiet

2 **T10.5b**

a The dragon gnawed Saint George's sword.
b I gave my aunt a lovely plant.
c He signed a cheque to buy the wreck.
d If you're in debt, you shouldn't bet.
e I fell on the quay and hurt my knee.
f We'll never know who wrote it, though.
g Please be quiet and don't start a riot!

Unit 11

1 The sounds /v/ and /w/, and silent *w*

1 **T11.1a**
- a There's something wrong with this veal.
- b Look at all those whales!
- c Now this is an old vine.
- d I'm sure it's in the west.
- e Can't you do something about that viper?

2

	1	2	3
A	west	whale	vine
B	veil	vet	west
C	vine	west	wet

T11.1b
- A What's in box A1?
- B Box A1 … er … 'west'.
- A What's in A2?
- B A2 … that's 'whale'.
- A What about A3?
- B 'Vine'.
- A B1?
- B 'Veil'.
- A Er … what about B2?
- B B2 … 'vet'.
- A And B3?
- B B3 … 'west'.
- A OK … now what's in box C1?
- B Box C1 … 'vine'.
- A And box C2?
- B Box C2 … 'west'.
- A Aha! And what about box C3? What's in that?
- B Box C3 … that's 'wet'.

4 **T11.1c**

1 whole 5 write
2 wrist 6 wrinkle
3 wreck 7 answer
4 sword 8 wrap

The word spelt out in the shaded column is 'wrestler'.

2 The sounds /b/ and /v/, and silent *b*

1 a *2 1* d *2 1* g *1 2*
 b *2 1* e *1 2* h *2 1*
 c *1 2* f *1 2*

5 lam~~b~~ de~~b~~t lumber
 num~~b~~ dou~~b~~t bombardment
 com~~b~~ su~~b~~tle combination
 lim~~b~~ thum~~b~~ number
 limbo dum~~b~~ plumber
 clim~~b~~ crum~~b~~ subtitle
 bom~~b~~ crumble

3 Weak forms with past conditionals

1 a 12 d 12 g 13 b 13 e 12 h 15
 c 14 f 11

2 **T11.3**
- a He might not have skidded if the road hadn't been icy.
- b If we'd been going much faster, we might all have been killed.
- c We couldn't have afforded it if he hadn't taken his credit card.
- d If they'd searched more carefully, they might have found the jewels.
- e Things would have been perfect if the engine hadn't caught fire.
- f If she'd gone by plane, it would have been simpler.
- g We wouldn't have crashed into him if he hadn't braked suddenly.
- h If I'd known what was going to happen, I probably wouldn't have gone.

3 would have /ˈwʊdəv/
 wouldn't have /ˈwʊdəntəv/
 might have /ˈmaɪtəv/
 might not have /ˈmaɪt nɒtəv/
 could have /ˈkʊdəv/
 couldn't have /ˈkʊdəntəv/

4 Sample story:
If I'd known what was going to happen, I probably wouldn't have gone. But I didn't know … and I went.
Just outside Vienna we hit some ice on the road, skidded, and crashed into the car in front. Well, maybe *we wouldn't have crashed into him if he hadn't braked suddenly.*
Frank, our driver, was really angry with himself. Of course *he might not have skidded if the road hadn't been icy.* Anyway, thanks to Frank we reached Vienna, but *if we'd been going much faster, we might all have been killed.*

4 Word linking in idiomatic expressions

2 **T11.4a**
- a Don't mention politics to my father – you know it's like a red rag to a bull!
- b Just say what you think – don't beat about the bush. I believe in being direct with people.
- c At the end of the film the villain came to a sticky end.
- d Yes, you're absolutely right! You've just put your finger on it. I couldn't agree with you more!
- e I wish I could remember her name! It's on the tip of my tongue …
- f I'll help you if you like, I'm at a loose end. Just call me when you need me!
- g Why do you fly off the handle whenever I mention our financial problems? It really doesn't help.
- h What's up with Vince? He's not himself.
- i What's Teresa been telling you about me? Whatever it is, take it with a pinch of salt.

3 he's head over heels in love with her = he's madly in love with her.
at the eleventh hour = at the last possible moment
day in, day out = every day, continuously
I've turned over a new leaf = I've started behaving better
he got out the wrong side of bed = he's been in a bad mood all day
they don't see eye to eye = they disagree or argue about something
it cost the earth = it was extremely expensive
he hit the roof = he got extremely angry

4 He's head over heels in love
   with her
      /j/
   a(t) the eleventh hour
      /j/   /j/
   day in, day out
   I've turned over a new leaf
   he got out of the wrong side of
      bed
           /j/   /w/
   they don't see eye to eye
              /j/
   it cos(t) the earth
   he hi(t) the roof

Unit 12

1 Sound symbol crossword puzzle

1

2 The name of the famous artist spelt out in the shaded column is Michelangelo Buonarotti.

2 Silent letter round-up

1 a handkerchief   g buoy
   b muscle   h corps
   c Wednesday   i Leicester
   d island   j handsome
   e sandwich   k ironing
   f leopard   l bruise

2 **T12.2b**
   A That's a nasty /'bru:ɪz/.
   B A bruise? /bru:z/

   A See you on /'wednezdeɪ/.
   B On Wednesday? /'wenzdeɪ/

   A She's got a pet /'li:əʊpɑ:rd/.
   B A pet leopard? /'lepəd/

   A He lives on an /'ɪzlænd/.
   B On an island? /'aɪlənd/

   A Have you been to /'laɪsester/?
   B To Leicester? /'lestə/

   A I hate doing the /'aɪrɒnɪŋg/.
   B The ironing? /'aɪənɪŋ/

3 Assimilation

1
   a /k/   /p/
      white gloves   white paper
         /k/   /p/
      white coffee   white magic
                            /p/
                         white bread
   b /g/   /b/
      red gold   red pepper
         /g/   /b/
      red carpet   red medicine
                            /b/
                         red-brick
   c /ŋ/   /m/
      green grass   green pepper
         /ŋ/   /m/
      green card   Green movement
                            /m/
                         green belt

Rules:
a /t/ changes to /k/ in front of /k/ and /g/ and to /p/ in front of /p/, /m/, and /b/.
b /d/ changes to /g/ in front of /k/ and /g/ and to /b/ in front of /p/, /m/, and /b/.
c /n/ changes to /ŋ/ in front of /k/ and /g/ and to /m/ in front of /p/, /m/, and /b/.

4 Emphatic forms

1 a We did win it.
   b He does get on my nerves.
   c I am sorry.
   d He did promise me.
   e They will be pleased.
   f I have missed you.
   g You are being childish.
   h Do grow up.
   i But I would like to get into films.
   j So where is Amy hiding?

T12.4
a A We didn't win the cup last year.
   B We did win it!
b A Listen to Ted. He's whistling in the bathroom again.
   B I know. Oooh. He does get on my nerves.
c A Look! You've just spilt wine on my sleeve.
   B Oh, I am sorry.
d A Will your father bring you something nice back from Brazil?
   B I hope so. He did promise me.
e A Look what I made for the children.
   B Oh, how lovely. They will be pleased.
f A Jenny, I'm home.
   B At last. Welcome home, darling. I have missed you.
g A Na na na na na.
   B Mum, tell Darren to shut up.
   C Oh, be quiet both of you. You are being childish.
h A Would Teddy-weddy like a drinky-winky?
   B Do grow up.
i A So you wouldn't like to be an accountant or a lawyer?
   B No. But I would like to get into films.
j A She isn't hiding in the cupboard or in the garden.
   B So where is Amy hiding?

5 Homophones

1 b fare / fair   e write / right
   c bare / bear   f allowed / aloud
   d sweet / suite

2 b *Whose* watch is this?
   c He used to be a *colonel* in the army.
   d The dog wagged its *tail* happily.
   e He isn't a town councillor, he's the *mayor* of the town.
   f The *guerillas* were armed with machine guns.
   g The lion gave a loud *roar* and then ran off.
   h The window's open and there's a terrible *draught* in here.